WICCA
FOR BEGINNERS

A GUIDE TO WICCAN BELIEFS, RITUALS, MAGIC & WITCHCRAFT

LISA CHAMBERLAIN

STERLING ETHOS
New York

STERLING ETHOS
New York

An Imprint of Sterling Publishing Co., Inc.
122 Fifth Avenue
New York, NY 10011

ISBN 978-1-4549-4084-5

Distributed in Canada by Sterling Publishing Co., Inc.
c/o Canadian Manda Group, 664 Annette Street
Toronto, Ontario, Canada M6S 2C8
Distributed in the United Kingdom by GMC Distribution Services
Castle Place, 166 High Street, Lewes, East Sussex, England BN7 1XU
Distributed in Australia by NewSouth Books
University of New South Wales, Sydney, NSW 2052, Australia

For information about custom editions, special sales, and premium and corporate
purchases, please contact Sterling Special Sales at 800-805-5489
or specialsales@sterlingpublishing.com.

Manufactured in Canada

6 8 10 9 7 5

sterlingpublishing.com

Design by Sharon Leigh Jacobs
Cover by Elizabeth M. Lindy
Picture credits—see page 158

=== **FOR ÁINE** ===

who gave me the inkling.

CONTENTS

PART THREE

WICCAN
MAGIC

PART FOUR

ADVICE FOR
ASPIRING WICCANS
& WITCHES

INTRODUCTION

I F YOU'RE READING THIS BOOK, YOU PROBABLY ALREADY KNOW that Witches and Wiccans are real people, living in the everyday world, and not the mean, green-faced, scary old hags seen in popular movies and Halloween costumes. They are not negative or malicious people, and they don't hex or try to manipulate others through devious means.

These stereotypes are a result of misconceptions about many ancient pagan religions found throughout Europe before the rise of Christianity, and while they may provide for good entertainment, they have also obscured the truth. Those who we would call the "witches" of the past were actually the healers, shamans, and wise people of their communities. They were respected and appreciated for the skills they utilized to benefit the greater good.

This doesn't mean that no one has ever used their abilities to harness natural forces in a self-serving or even nefarious manner. After all, since the dawn of humanity, there has always been the *potential* for selfish and destructive acts in every person. But Wicca has nothing to do with any sort of service-to-self mentality. On the contrary, Wicca (along with many other forms of Witchcraft) is rooted in the understanding that we are all interconnected—with each other, and with the Earth that sustains us. Wicca is a spiritual practice that allows people to reclaim the balanced relationship with Nature that our modern world has become largely disconnected from.

For a long time, Wicca was mostly practiced in secrecy, whether by covens gathering privately for holiday rituals or by solitary Witches marking the passing of the seasons with their own personal celebrations. This is still the case for many Wiccans, whether due to the negative stereotypes mentioned above, or simply because they prefer to keep their spiritual lives private.

However, times have certainly changed. As societal attitudes have become more open-minded regarding alternative spiritual paths, Wicca has attracted an unprecedented explosion of interest—on a level that those of us old enough to remember life before the internet would never have imagined possible. A few decades ago, people curious about Wicca typically had little access to credible information, especially those without a good New Age or occult bookstore anywhere in the vicinity. Today, you can simply enter "Wicca" into an online search engine and spend whole days, weeks, or even years exploring the results.

Of course, not all websites, articles, and books are of equal quality, and the sheer amount of available information about Wicca can be overwhelming, especially since many sources present conflicting information. Since Wicca is a thoroughly decentralized religion, with no agreed-upon authoritative text or standard set of traditions, you will find an enormous variety of perspectives, philosophies, and beliefs among practicing Wiccans, some of which will likely resonate with you more than others.

You are always advised to explore the ideas and practices that make the most intuitive sense to you and let go of whatever doesn't *feel* right. Just as your knowing, inner self brought you to this particular book, it will guide you throughout your exploration of Wicca, whether you decide to pursue this spiritual path or simply satisfy your curiosity and move on.

This guide is intended as a brief introduction to the spiritual movement known as Wicca. We'll start with an attempt to define what is in reality a widely diverse set of beliefs and practices, focusing on the core foundations that its various traditions hold in common. Then, we'll move on to an overview of Wiccan rituals and magical practices, including an overview of the most-often used ritual tools and magical ingredients. Finally, you'll find insights and tips for pursuing your interest in Wicca further, should you so desire, along with an example ritual and a beginner-friendly spell for you to try. And as with all of my books, you'll also find a suggested reading list for learning more about the rich world of Wicca.

By the end of this book you will have a solid sense of what Wicca is all about. I hope you enjoy the journey!

Blessed Be.

PART ONE

WHAT IS WICCA?

A LIVING, EVOLVING
SPIRITUAL PATH

ONE OF THE FIRST THINGS TO KNOW ABOUT WICCA IS THAT IT is not an organized religion. That is to say, there is no single sacred text that all Wiccans follow, no official leaders to make decisions about which practices are accepted or required, and no official place of worship within any given community for Wiccans to attend. Instead, Wicca is a decentralized set of spiritual beliefs and practices that have several core elements in common, but which may look quite different from one practitioner to another, or from one coven to the next.

There are many different forms and traditions of Wicca—somewhat like the various sects or denominations of organized religions—which have developed and evolved over time as more and more people have discovered this realm of spirituality. However, each coven and each individual is still independent of others, and has a different approach when it comes to practicing Wicca. Even covens within established traditions, however, operate independently of one another, and may have differing interpretations of the beliefs and practices within the overarching tradition. As for those who practice on their own, whether within a tradition or in a more eclectic fashion, it's likely that no two practices are ever exactly alike.

And Wicca continues to evolve with each new generation that embraces the path. It seems today that non-traditional, eclectic practices are quickly becoming the norm, but many traditional, more structured forms of Wicca are thriving as well.

What all this means is that you have the absolute freedom to craft your very own personalized practice of Wicca, if you wish, as you explore and develop your connection to the Universal energies that make up all of creation. Alternatively, you can seek out an established coven (or more informal group) of Traditional Wiccans to learn from and adopt their practices. You might even try a little bit of both. It is entirely up to you.

What this level of freedom also means, however, is that you're likely to encounter some disagreement among different practitioners about what Wicca is or isn't, what this path entails, what it excludes, who is "truly" Wiccan, and who is not. Wiccans can sometimes be an argumentative bunch—as anyone passionate about their religion can be—and this certainly includes Wiccan authors!

The purpose of this guide, however, is not to try to sway you toward one belief, tradition, or approach over another, but to present you with a basic orientation to the origins of Wicca, its core beliefs and concepts, and some examples of what this path can look like in practice. Where you go from there is, again, completely up to you.

To that end, we'll begin now with a basic description of the religion of Wicca, and what it means to be (or not be) a "Witch" with a capital *W*. We'll then take a brief look at the history of Wicca's development in the mid-twentieth century, before diving into the core beliefs at the heart of this fascinating religion.

THE OLD RELIGION

WICCA IS CONSIDERED AN EARTH-CENTERED RELIGION. Its focus is on reverence for the natural world and the cycles of birth, growth, change, death and rebirth experienced by all living beings. Our interconnectedness with Nature is something our earliest ancestors were aware of, without question, and Wicca's emphasis on this relationship is a revival of an older, pre-Christian spirituality that has existed in one form or another in cultures around the globe since the beginning of recorded history. These ancient belief systems are at the root of what Wiccans and many other Witches and Pagans call "the Old Religion." But while it may draw much of its inspiration from the spiritual practices of our pagan ancestors, Wicca itself is a modern religion of relatively recent origins, as we will see later on.

Among the many aspects of Wicca that distinguish it from other, more widely recognized religions is its emphasis on the divine feminine, in addition to the more familiar divine masculine. Wicca has none of the patriarchy often found in other Western faiths—instead, there is an equal gender polarity between the divine masculine and divine feminine, represented by the God and the Goddess. These two co-creative archetypes are the spiritual embodiments of all natural forces and processes, and each has their own particular domains in the form of masculine and feminine energies.

The Goddess is recognized as embodying the Earth itself, as well as the Moon. The God, as her counterpart, is embodied by the Sun and its nourishing light. When speaking of Wicca generally, these deities are unnamed, but individual covens and solitary practitioners may have specific names for the God and the Goddess. These names typically come from pre-Christian cultures, whose various gods and goddesses are often seen as individual representatives, or "aspects," of the all-encompassing divine masculine and feminine. Traditionally, Wiccans worked consistently with one masculine aspect of the God and one feminine aspect of the Goddess, but many eclectic practitioners today incorporate several different ancient deities into their practice.

For Wiccans, the passing of time is an inherent function of Nature, and it is revered and celebrated at regular points throughout the Wiccan calendar, also known as the Wheel of the Year. Rooted in the natural cycles of the seasons, which were an integral part of daily life for our ancestors who lived off the land, the Wheel marks the turning points of each season according to the Sun's position in the sky (relative to the Earth) and the completion of each cycle of the Moon. On these occasions, Wiccans honor the God and the Goddess through ritual, feasting, and celebration.

But this reverence for the natural cycles of time and the ever-turning of the Wheel is also lived every day, as Wiccans intentionally appreciate the warmth of the rising Sun, the nourishing abundance of the food on their plates, the beauty of a freshly fallen snow, or the healing properties of the herbs growing in their gardens. In these and many other ways, Wiccans stay spiritually connected to the energies of Nature and the timeless wisdom of the ancestors, even as they live and enjoy their modern lives.

As noted earlier, Wicca has been classified as an Earth-centered religion, but a few additional descriptors can help define it within the context of other, somewhat similar spiritual paths.

First, as a nature-based collection of beliefs and practices, Wicca is considered to be a form of paganism. "Paganism" is an umbrella term that has been defined in the broadest sense as any religion that isn't Christianity, Judaism, or Islam. The word "pagan" comes from the Latin word for "country person," and initially had no religious context. However, it was used later in a negative manner when the Roman Empire sought to stamp out the old beliefs and practices of agrarian peoples throughout Europe.

Today, the words *pagan* and *paganism* are often capitalized to distinguish the many modern Pagan religions and spiritual practices (alternatively referred to as Neopaganism) from the more general uses of the word. Some Wiccans resist the term and draw a clear distinction between themselves and Pagans with a capital *P*, but from a historical and cultural standpoint, Wicca is indeed a pagan religion.

Wicca is also considered a shamanic religion. *Shamanism* is a term originally used to refer to ancient religions found in regions of Asia, but it has since been used in reference to many indigenous traditions throughout the world whose origins predate written history. In fact, shamanism is often called the world's first religion. Shamans were the first "medicine people" and were revered in their societies.

Shamanic traditions involve an element of *animism*—the belief that seemingly inanimate natural objects, such as rocks and trees, are as infused with spiritual energy as any person or animal. Shamanic practitioners may achieve altered states of consciousness through ritual dance, drumming, breath work, or other energetic means, through which they can interact with the spirit world.

In indigenous communities, shamans brought back the knowledge found on these "journeys" to use for healing and the general well-being of the community.

Like shamans, Wiccans understand that there is a conscious energy running throughout the Earth and the cosmos beyond. They seek connection with the unseen spirits of the natural world, achieved through rituals in which energy is raised for this purpose. They may also work with the spiritual energy of natural agents like crystals, stones, and/or herbs for healing, wisdom, and protection. Their methods often draw from a combination of ancestral wisdom (whether passed down or rediscovered) and their own intuitive approach to this co-creative relationship with Nature.

Depending on whom you ask, Wicca is also considered a duotheistic, polytheistic, and/or pantheistic religion. These terms simply identify different concepts of deity within belief systems, and since Wicca is a decentralized system with many variations, all three terms can apply.

Wiccans whose focus is solely on the God and the Goddess, with no other, "lesser," deities included in their cosmology, are considered duotheists; those who incorporate other ancient deities in addition to the God and Goddess are polytheists. Pantheism is the belief that a deity, or "God," is present in all things, and that there is no separation between the divine and what we perceive as "reality." These and other classifications can be applied to Wicca, depending on the individual practitioner's perspective, and are the subject of much lively debate among the Wiccan community.

Finally, although Wicca can be categorized in all of these different ways, some still question whether it is, technically speaking, a "religion." The answer, at least from a legal standpoint, is "yes." Although it may be far less visible than organized religions like Judaism, Christianity, or Islam, Wicca has been recognized by

US courts as being entitled to the same religious protections and is even included in the chaplain's handbook of the US Army.

The rise in the number of practitioners during the second half of the twentieth century was no doubt a factor in this legal designation. It has been estimated that close to one million people around the world identify as Wiccans, with the majority found in the US and the UK. Whatever the actual count might be, it's clear that the numbers are rising steadily in the twenty-first century, as more knowledge about the religion becomes available and widely shared.

Nonetheless, there are many Wiccans who, for various reasons, dislike the concept of "religion" and prefer terms like "spiritual path" or "belief system." Those drawn to Wicca tend to have a nonconformist approach to life, and therefore may not be comfortable with the connotations of dogma and structure that the word "religion" can evoke. So although there are benefits to having Wicca legally recognized as a religion, the choice of whether to think of it as one is up to the individual.

Wiccans, Witches, and the Capital *W*

Of course, the terms we've just discussed are not the only ones that Wiccans have differing perspectives on. (As noted earlier, there's probably very little that all Wiccans would completely agree on, but that's to be expected in such a dynamic and individualized realm of spirituality!) Perhaps one of the biggest questions newcomers tend to have is whether a Wiccan is the same thing as a Witch. The answer, which should come as no surprise by now, is "yes and no."

The terms *Witch* and *Wiccan* are often used interchangeably, and in many contexts they do mean the same thing. However, it's important to note that there are Wiccans who identify as Witches, and Wiccans who don't. (There are also plenty of Witches who don't identify as Wiccans, but who may hold similar beliefs and follow some of the same practices as Wiccans.) Typically, this distinction is due to differing perspectives on the word "witchcraft."

Witchcraft, like *paganism*, is a catchall term that has been applied to certain spiritual activities from an outsider's perspective, rather than a term the practitioners themselves might have used. Anthropologists and others have applied this word to various practices, including medicinal healing, prayer, shamanic journeying, folk magic, and, in the past, any phenomenon (usually negative) that people couldn't understand or attribute to logical causes.

Also like *paganism*, the term *witchcraft* came into use as a way of distinguishing the good (i.e. Christianity) from the bad (i.e. everything else). Yet it, too, has been coopted in modern times by those who consider themselves Witches. In this context, *Witchcraft* is often capitalized, and the term represents a broad array of beliefs and practices with roots in pre-Christian cultures.

Wicca is, technically speaking, a form of witchcraft, and was even called *witchcraft* by its twentieth-century founders, as we will see shortly. Many of its practitioners refer to Wicca as "the Craft," particularly when referring to associated practices like magic, which we will examine in part three (see pages 109–35). Furthermore, the words *witch* and *wicca* are linguistically related, as *wicca* was the Old English word that later became *witch*.

Nonetheless, some Wiccans are uncomfortable with the negative connotations, however inaccurate, surrounding the *W* word. These are typically practitioners who don't use any form of magic outside of Sabbat and Esbat rituals. They draw a distinction between Wicca as a spiritual practice and individual relationship with the divine, and witchcraft as a practice that is not necessarily spiritual. The beauty of Wicca's decentralized and individualized nature is that these Wiccans are perfectly entitled to this viewpoint, and no agreement with the Witches of the larger Wiccan community is necessary!

However, many Wiccans do blend magic into their practice to varying degrees—enough so that both ritual and magic are combined in many Wiccan books and resources, including this guide. The terms *Wiccan* and *Witch* may be used interchangeably in the context of practices that are found in Witchcraft generally, but *Wiccan* is used for specifically Wiccan beliefs and practices.

Finally, while it's standard to capitalize the word *Wicca* (and, therefore, *Wiccan*), there are currently no established conventions when it comes to *witch* and *witchcraft*. Some practitioners feel no need to capitalize these more general terms, but others see it as a means of cultivating cultural acceptance of the wider world of Witchcraft in the twenty-first century. In the spirit of respect for those who feel strongly about honoring Wicca, Witchcraft, and the role of the Witch in modern society, this guide uses the capital *W* for all three terms.

One Name, Many Paths

Whether you consider it a religion, a belief system, or a spiritual path, the phenomenon known as Wicca has many different forms and expressions. There are very formalized approaches involving hierarchical structures within covens; looser, more egalitarian Wiccan groups or "circles"; and solitary practitioners, who may follow a particular tradition or an eclectic blend of traditions and independent innovations.

The oldest form of what we now call Wicca began with a coven of Witches, with elaborately ritualized practices, in which some members would rise through degrees of initiation to become High Priestesses and Priests. Some covens today closely follow these original practices, the details of which remain secret from all but initiated members. These covens trace their initiatory lineage back to the first covens of the mid-1900s, and their practices are now known as Traditional Wicca (or British Traditional Wicca).

Other covens have moved away from Traditional Wicca to varying extents, adapting their practices and even inventing new ones, and often incorporating more egalitarian structures. These are typically known as eclectic covens, as they draw their inspiration from many different sources and traditions. Wiccan circles tend to be in the eclectic camp as well, with more open membership and less expectation of conformity to a specific set of practices.

There are also an untold number of solitary Witches who prefer to practice alone. They may follow, as best they can, the practices of one of the paths within Traditional Wicca, or they may be eclectics. Eclectic Wicca is where the variations are most apparent, particularly in the area of duotheism vs. polytheism, and where there is the most flexibility for interpreting the templates of Wiccan beliefs and practices through the lens of personal intuition.

But to better understand Wicca's blending of the ancient and modern, let's take a brief look at its origins, its spread from Britain to the wider world, and its ultimate evolution into a highly diversified spiritual practice.

WICCAN HISTORY:
FACTS AND MYSTERY

WICCA'S HISTORY IS FULL OF INTERESTING AND UNUSUAL characters who made various contributions to this spiritual movement over the course of the twentieth century. However, its origins can be traced back to the late nineteenth century, during the British occult movement. The word *occult* refers to all manner of mystical, magical, or "supernatural" pursuits, such as astrology, alchemy, psychic mediumship, and other elements of what is now called the Western Mystery Tradition. Several secret societies existed in Britain at this time, in which occult scholars could learn from each other, and many of their discoveries were of interest to later generations of occult enthusiasts.

One such enthusiast was Gerald Gardner (1884–1964), who is widely credited with the founding of what we now call Wicca. Gardner had become interested in a theory advanced in the early 1920s by anthropologist Margaret Murray (1863–1963), about a pagan religion that could be traced back to ancient times. Murray believed that this religion had been largely obliterated during the Middle Ages, but some small, secret remnants managed to survive the Christianization of Europe. She called this religion a "witch cult" and asserted that its practitioners were organized into thirteen-member groups, or covens, and worshipped a male "horned" god.

In the early 1940s, Gardner's exploration of mystical and occult experiences inspired him to develop a new incarnation of the witch cult. He had met a group of Witches who he believed were practicing the original "Old Religion," described by Murray and others, and then formed his own coven, Bricket Wood, modeled in part on what he learned from them. Blending their practices with ideas from within the Western Mystery Tradition, such as Freemasonry and ceremonial magic, Gardner's version of Witchcraft expanded the deity worship to include a female goddess along with the male god.

In 1947, Gardner met and befriended Aleister Crowley (1875–1947), a well-known occultist and writer who had explored and participated in many religious and esoteric traditions from around the world, including Buddhism, Jewish mysticism, Hinduism, the Tarot, astrology, and more. Crowley's writings had a significant influence on Gardner, who included some of the rituals devised by Crowley in his own practices. It was Crowley who coined the spelling of *magick* with a *k*, to distinguish his form of magic from the "stage magic" of illusionists.

Crowley is a complicated figure for many Wiccans today, as some of the practices he engaged in were considered quite scandalous, and his part in the history of the religion helped perpetuate an incorrect association between Witchcraft and Satanism. (It is important to note that Satanism is part of the Christian worldview, not a Pagan concept. Wicca has nothing to do with Satanism or any other practice that isn't in alignment with balance, harmony, and respect for the well-being of all.) Furthermore, Crowley had a reputation for being misogynist and racist, attitudes incompatible with the Wiccan way of life.

The tradition now known as Gardnerian Wicca began to flourish as Gardner brought other interested occultists into his coven including several women, one of whom was Doreen Valiente (1922–99). Valiente became the High Priestess of Bricket Wood in the early 1950s and revised much of the original material the coven had been using, in part because she felt it had too much of Crowley's influence. Eventually, Valiente parted ways with Gardner over his decisions to speak to the press about Witchcraft, and to limit the power of women in the coven in response to their criticisms.

Valiente formed her own coven in 1957 and went on to study Witchcraft with other leading figures in the movement. Ultimately she wrote several influential books that helped launch the evolution of Witchcraft from a secret society phenomenon into a widespread practice. Other leading figures in the expansion of the Craft were Alex Sanders (1926–88), who founded the Alexandrian Tradition, and Raymond Buckland (1934–2017), who formed the Seax-Wica Tradition in the early 1970s and is credited with bringing Gardnerian Wicca to the United States.

The "official" history of Wicca, as well as the broader occult movement, is well-documented by many scholars and practitioners. Just a tiny glimpse of that complex and sprawling story is offered here. If you'd like to learn more, you might want to start with the short list of recommended references on page 154–55.

Timeless, but Not Quite So Ancient

Despite the claims of Gardner and others to have discovered and revived an authentic ancient tradition, academic historians never could find much factual evidence to support the "witch-cult" theory. While there is plenty of evidence of nature-based deity worship and magical practices among various pagan pre-Christian cultures, there's nothing to really suggest the existence of a single religion transcending geography and culture across the European continent. Eventually, the "ancient lineage" myth about Wicca's origins was essentially debunked.

Yet interest in and practice of Wicca continues to grow. Perhaps this is because, even though we may only know fragments of the past, we do know that there was something, some energetic force

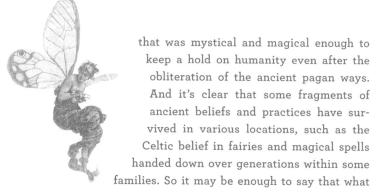

that was mystical and magical enough to keep a hold on humanity even after the obliteration of the ancient pagan ways. And it's clear that some fragments of ancient beliefs and practices have survived in various locations, such as the Celtic belief in fairies and magical spells handed down over generations within some families. So it may be enough to say that what the original founders of modern Wicca did was create new forms through which people could tap into timeless realms, bridging the gap between the ancient and modern worlds with new expressions of a magical energy that has always existed.

Claiming "Wicca" in the Twenty-First Century

As we have seen, the second half of the twentieth century brought Wicca (as well as other forms of Witchcraft) from England to the rest of the United Kingdom, to the United States, and ultimately to the rest of the English-speaking world. With these migrations came several changes to the original Gardnerian beliefs and practices, and entirely new forms were created, including Dianic, Celtic, and Georgian traditions, as well as eclectic practices adapted from a range of existing forms.

Over the decades, many an argument has been made over what truly constitutes "Wicca," especially now that so many people practice it in so many different ways. And since there is no authoritative body to grant official "inclusion" into the religion, there's a lot of leeway in terms of who might "claim" to be Wiccan.

One particular distinction that followers of Gardnerian and Gardnerian-inspired Traditions often draw between themselves and other Wiccans is the concept of "lineage." Gardner performed rituals of initiation to formally admit new people to the secrets of the Craft. As Gardnerian Wicca grew and evolved, members of the Bricket Wood coven went on to form other covens and initiated new Witches into the tradition. Offshoots of Gardenian Wicca adopted this practice as well, so that today's Traditional Witches can often trace their initiatory lineage back to the early origins of Wicca, as we saw earlier.

Yet as information and new ideas about Wicca and other Witchcraft spread, the requirements of initiation and lineage became less absolute, and the options of self-initiation and solitary practice became popular for people who were interested in the Craft but were unable (or unwilling) to join or start a coven. From the Traditionalist point of view, this departure from the old ways has led to a pervasive idea that Wicca is "anything you want it to be," with little to no understanding of its original forms among the newer generations of practitioners.

Though there is much to support this argument, eclectics and other non-Traditionalists see things differently. For one thing, the flexibility and adaptability that draws so many to the religion was actually part of its inception. Gardner's original material was based on a combination of other, preexisting sources, and was revised and added to throughout his own time. He was observed to have told his own coveners that they should treat the Book of Shadows (his name for the collected material used in ritual and magical practice) not as a permanent text, but as something to add to and alter for themselves as they saw fit.

Furthermore, Gardner and his fellow Witches didn't use the term *Wicca* as an identifying term, but rather called their practice "Witchcraft," "the Craft," or "the Old Religion." Gardner did refer to the members of his tradition collectively as "The Wica," but "Wicca" as a name for the religion didn't come into regular use until the 1960s, when it spread to the United States and Australia. In fact, many Gardnerian Witches, who consider their tradition to be "pre-Wiccan," don't identify as Wiccan at all!

This debate within the wider Wiccan community may never be resolved, given that it is almost as old as Wicca itself. Nonetheless, all forms of the Craft have something in common at their core: an affinity with older, pre-Christian spiritual practices that may not be well documented in written history but have retained a place in the human imagination. Indeed, "the Old Religion" isn't found in a particular tradition, coven, or practice, but is an energetic presence underlying all of Wicca.

CORE BELIEFS OF WICCAN TRADITIONS

FOR ALL OF THE VARIATIONS THAT ARE FOUND ACROSS contemporary Wiccan beliefs and practices, there are still important core tenets that those who identify as Wiccans acknowledge. The beliefs described here stem in part from the developments of Gardner and others in the British Traditional Witchcraft movement, but also from other strands of pre-Christian cultural practice and aspects of the Western Mystery Tradition.

Imagine an existence before "modern civilization" as we know it. There is no electricity, no running water, no telephone communication, and no internet (gasp!). You can't get bananas in a supermarket in January while living thousands of miles from the nearest tropical fruit farm. There are no books, magazines, or newspapers. No weather forecasts, no news bulletins or alarms to warn of tornadoes, blizzards, or hurricanes. No calendars to mark the passing of the months, and no clocks to mark the passing of the days. And, perhaps most significantly, no environmental destruction anywhere near the scale we've been witnessing for the past few hundred years. Just the land, the water, and the sky.

Our oldest ancestors lived in this world. They shared an intimate connection with the Earth and the elements in a way we couldn't imagine today. They received information directly from the natural world and its continually turning seasons. Through the bounty of the Earth and the forces of rain, sun, air, and fire, they participated in the natural cycles of life.

They harvested the Earth's wild abundance to make food and medicine, and they worked with the Earth intentionally to create growth through crops and livestock. In the millennia before what we've come to call the Information Age, they learned what they needed to know about the world and its wonders from what their surroundings taught them. To survive their primitive circumstances, they had to pay attention.

And pay attention they did! Ruins of ancient monuments around the world demonstrate the sophisticated knowledge that our ancestors gained from studying the sky. For example, the Mayans incorporated observations of the cycles of the Moon and Venus into their calendar systems. In Ireland, a Stone Age farming community built a temple mound—known today as Newgrange—with a passage that is illuminated only by the rising Sun at the Winter Solstice.

These accomplishments didn't arise solely out of close study, however, but were created in the context of a spiritual relationship with the cosmos. Mayan myths credit the god Itzamná with giving them the knowledge of the calendar system. The origins of Newgrange are less well documented, but the many ancient carvings found among its stones—particularly the triple spiral at its entrance—suggest an understanding of Universal energies that went beyond basic astronomical knowledge.

Wicca draws on the primal energy of the relationship to the natural world, and although the world has been dramatically transformed over time by the impact of human civilizations, Wiccans know that our most essential requirements for survival have not changed. We still need the Earth, and we still benefit from living in balance with Nature and with each other.

In this spirit, Wicca comprises beliefs and traditions from two chief sources: what is known about our ancestors' ways of life, and what is imagined, both collectively and individually. The continuity with the ancient pagan world may be considered sym-

bolic rather than literal, but in grounding their worldview in the realities of nature as our ancestors did, Wiccans create a life of attunement with the primal energies of the Universe.

The Deities of Wicca

As we saw earlier, Wicca embraces the existence of two main deities, who are generically called the God and the Goddess (or, in some traditions, the Lord and the Lady). These two deities are, according to Wiccans, the original feminine and masculine forces of nature that make all life possible.

Some eclectic Wiccans may, in their spiritual orientation to the divine, favor the masculine aspect of deity over the feminine to a degree, while others, especially followers of Dianic and other feminist forms of Wicca, pay far more attention to the feminine. Whatever the case, in its most basic form the relationship is between equals, as both feminine and masculine energies make up life on Earth. In the natural world, one cannot exist without the other.

As such, representations of the Goddess and the God tend to symbolize aspects of the life, death, and rebirth cycles that correspond to feminine and masculine realms. The God is not only associated with the Sun, but also very often referred to and depicted as the Horned God of the forest. The Goddess, when associated with the Moon, is actually comprised of three aspects—the Maiden, the Mother, and the Crone—represented by the stages of the lunar cycle. Yet the Goddess is also embodied by the fertility of the Earth.

Some Wiccans experience these deities as unnamed energetic presences, referring to them simply as "the God" and "the Goddess." Others, as mentioned earlier, have individual names for them, which typically come from pagan cultures of the past. Those whose practice incorporates ancient deities typically experience them as individual aspects of the Goddess and God, with their own historical, mythological, and spiritual significance among the cultures where they originated.

In Traditional Wicca, covens often center their worship and affiliations on one god and goddess as aspects of the deities. Coveners may have their own personal alignments with other deities of their choosing, but in formal ritual will work with the deities the coven is devoted to. In eclectic practices, many different gods and goddesses may represent the Goddess and God. Furthermore, other deities can be part of Wiccan ritual in their own right, in addition to the traditional, or "supreme" deities.

THE HORNED GOD/THE SUN GOD

Across many pre-Christian European cultures, a common archetype appears known as the Horned God, who is the ruler of wild animals and the hunting activities of humans. As a symbol of his connection with the animals of the forests and plains, he is often depicted with horns or antlers on his head. Deities who represent the God in this archetypal form include the Greek god Pan and the Celtic god Cernunnos.

The God is also the ruler of the Sun, whose light and heat make life possible. In this aspect, it is his yearlong journey around the Earth that forms the basis for the Wiccan calendar, which we will discuss shortly. Many ancient deities associated with the Sun may be linked with this aspect of the God, such as Lugh (Celtic), Ra (Egyptian), and Apollo (Greek). As the masculine, or projective, energy of procreation, the God is also associated with sex. He is often represented in phallic symbols, such as the previously mentioned horns, as well as spears, swords, wands, and arrows.

If the God, as the Sun, is the projective energy of all life, the Goddess, as the Earth, is the receptive energy that sustains life and allows it to flourish. Her realm of influence includes the Earth and its oceans, as well as the Moon that creates the tides. As a nurturing and tending essence, she is also associated with domesticated animals. She is known in some traditions as the Great Mother.

As the female force that sustains life, the Goddess is represented by three aspects, which mirror both the stages of a woman's reproductive life and the waxing, full, and waning phases of the Moon. Some representations from ancient societies show her as having three faces, one representing each aspect. In some Wiccan traditions, she is called the Triple Moon Goddess, while others call her simply the Triple Goddess. Whatever she is called, each aspect of the Goddess has its role in the life cycle of the Earth and its inhabitants, including the inner life of each human being.

Symbols associated with the Goddess reflect the receptive energy of sex, such as the cup and cauldron, as well as her gifts of abundance, such as flowers and fruits. In various Wiccan cosmologies the Goddess may be represented by the Greek Diana, the Egyptian Isis, and the Celtic Brigid, among others.

THE MAIDEN

The Goddess in her Maiden aspect aligns with the crescent phase of the Moon. She represents the growth phase of life, reflected in the waxing of the Moon as it moves toward fullness. She is also associated with the season of Spring and with youth, innocence, and independence. Goddesses representing the Maiden include the Greek goddesses Persephone and Artemis, the Celtic Rhiannon, and the Nordic Freya.

THE MOTHER

When the Moon waxes to full, the Goddess is in her Mother aspect, the source of the Earth's abundance. She's associated with Summer, the lush time of year when plant and animal life mature into fullness. This is considered by many Witches to be the most powerful aspect of the Goddess. The Mother is represented by the Greek Demeter and Selene, the Roman Ceres, and the Celtic Badb and Danu, among others.

THE CRONE

The waning Moon belongs to the Crone Goddess, who is a symbol of death—a necessary part of the life cycle—and of the wisdom gained from a full and productive life. She is associated with Autumn and Winter, the winding down and ending of the growing season. She completes the cycle of the Moon and the cycle of death, as well as the rebirth in all living things. The cycle begins again at the New Moon when the Maiden returns. Goddesses associated with death and the underworld often represents her, such as the Greek Hecate, the Russian Baba Yaga, and the Celtic Morrigan and Cailleach Bear.

LVNA

THE WHEEL OF
THE YEAR

WICCA IS CALLED AN "EARTH-CENTERED" RELIGION IN PART because its worship traditions follow the turning of the seasons. In an age when we are removed from nature by technological advances and endless distractions, marking the Wheel of the Year becomes a way to reconnect with the Divine essence of life and the Earth's role in our existence. Some Witches refer to their participation in the Wiccan holidays as "Turning the Wheel," to emphasize our co-creative relationship with nature. The eight major holidays, known as Sabbats, are considered "days of power" and are marked by Wiccans and other Witches and Pagans of many traditions. There are also monthly rituals marking each lunar cycle, known as Esbats—referred to by some as the "second Wheel of the Year."

The Wiccan year does not follow the standard Gregorian calendar, which begins on January 1. Instead, it follows the seasons, marking the progress in the Earth's path around the Sun (which appears, to be the Sun's journey around the Earth) and the corresponding changes to life on Earth. Four of the eight Sabbats are "solar holidays": Winter and Summer Solstices, and the Spring and Autumn Equinoxes. The other four are the "Earth festivals," which occur near the "cross-quarter days" between the solar Sabbats, and are based on older pagan folk festivals linked to the life cycles of animals and agriculture.

The existence of eight Sabbats, rather than four, illustrates that the conventional delineations between the four seasons are somewhat artificial. For example, Spring does not suddenly turn into Summer on June 21, when the Sun reaches its zenith in the sky. Typically, the weather has been warming up for a good few weeks before the conventional calendar calls it "Summer." (In fact, the ancient Celts recognized Beltane, on May 1, as the start of Summer!) As we will soon see, the four cross-quarter Sabbats mark the "seasons in-between seasons" and, together with the solar Sabbats, guide us through the never-ending transitions of the Wheel of the Year.

Over the course of the year, the Sabbats of the Wheel tell a mythical story about the relationship between the Goddess and the God, which is one of both mother and child and co-creative consorts. The stages of each overlapping relationship parallel the seasonal and agricultural cycles that were crucial for the survival of rural communities. The God, as the Sun, is born, grows strong, and ultimately dies in order to be reborn again. The Goddess, as the Earth, is both mother and partner to the God, and goes through her own cycles of youth, motherhood, and old age as the seasons turn. These cycles are honored more explicitly at the Esbats, as we will see below.

In the following descriptions, the dates for the solar Sabbats are given as a range, to account for differences in the Sun's position in the sky relative to where one lives. For the Earth festivals, the standard date is given; however, many practitioners mark the beginning of the holiday after sundown on the evening before. Obviously, those living in the Southern Hemisphere follow the Wheel in the opposite direction, so that Beltane is on October 31, for example.

THE SABBATS

YULE

WINTER SOLSTICE
DECEMBER 20-23

Considered in most Wiccan traditions to be the beginning of the year, Yule is a celebration of the rebirth of the God. It is the shortest day of the year, offering a welcome reminder that even though the cold season is still just getting underway, it doesn't last forever, as the days will begin to lengthen again after this point. This is a festive holiday celebrating light, as well as preparation for a time of quiet, inner focus as the Earth rests from her labor.

The word *yule* is derived from midwinter festivals celebrated by ancient Germanic tribes. "Yule" is still referenced in modern Christmas carols, and many of the traditions surrounding the Christian holiday, such as wreaths, Christmas trees, and caroling, have their roots in these pagan traditions. (It was common for the Christian churches to "adopt" pagan holidays, repurposing them for celebrating saints or important events, as a way of drawing people away from their indigenous religions.)

≡ I Ꮇ Ᏼ O Ꮮ C ≡

FEBRUARY 2

Imbolc marks the first stirrings of Spring as the long months of Winter are nearly past. The Goddess is beginning her recovery after the birth of the God, and the lengthening days signal the strengthening of the God's power. Seeds begin to germinate, daffodils appear, and hibernating animals start to emerge from their slumber. It is a time for ritual cleansing from the long period of inactivity. Covens may perform initiation rites at this time of new beginnings.

The name Imbolc is derived from an Old Irish term for the pregnancy of ewes and has been sometimes translated as meaning "ewe's milk," in reference to the birthing of the first lambs of the season. It is also called Candlemas, and sometimes Brigid's Day in Irish traditions. Associated with the beginnings of growth, it's also considered a festival of the Maiden.

═OSTARA═

SPRING EQUINOX
MARCH 19-21

At the Spring Equinox, light and dark are finally equal again, and growth accelerates as both the light from the still-young God of the Sun and the fertility of the Goddess of the Earth grow more powerful. Gardening begins in earnest and trees send out blossoms to participate with the pollinating bees. The equal length of day and night brings about a time for balancing and bringing opposing forces into harmony.

The name Ostara comes from the Saxon Eostre, a Germanic goddess of Spring and renewal. This is where the name Easter comes from, another example of the Christian church's pattern of co-opting pagan traditions.

⇥ BELTANE ⇤

MAY 1

As Spring begins to move into Summer, the Goddess is making her transition into the Mother aspect, and the God matures into his full potency. Beltane is a fire festival, and a celebration of love, sex, and reproduction. It's at this time that the Goddess couples with the God to ensure his rebirth after his death at the end of the life cycle. Fertility is at its height and the Earth prepares to flourish with new life.

The name Beltane comes from an ancient festival celebrated throughout the Celtic Isles that marked the beginning of Summer and is derived from an old Celtic word meaning "bright fire." The ancient Irish would light giant fires to purify and protect their cattle; and jumping over fires was considered a way to increase fertility and luck in the coming season.

LITHA

SUMMER SOLSTICE
JUNE 20-22

Long considered one of the most magical times of the year, the Summer Solstice sees the God and the Goddess at the peak of their powers. The Sun is at its highest point and the days are at their longest. This is a celebration of the abundance of sunlight and warmth, and the physical manifestation of abundance as the year heads toward the first of the harvests. It's a time of ease and of brief rest after the work of planting and before the work of harvesting begins.

Some traditions call this Sabbat Litha, a name traced back to an old Anglo-Saxon word for this time of year.

≡ LAMMAS ≡

AUGUST 1

Lammas marks the beginning of the harvest season. The first crops are brought in from the fields, the trees and plants begin dropping their fruits and seeds, and the days are growing shorter as the God's power begins to wane. This is a time for giving thanks for the abundance of the growing season as it begins to wind down.

The word Lammas stems from an old Anglo-Saxon word pairing meaning "loaf mass," and it was customary to bless fresh loaves of bread as a way of celebrating the harvest. Lammas is alternately known as Lughnasa, after the traditional festivals in Ireland and Scotland held at this time to honor the Celtic god Lugh, who was associated with the Sun.

⇒ MABON ⇐

AUTUMN EQUINOX
SEPTEMBER 21-24

The harvest season is still in focus at the Autumn Equinox. The animals born during the year have matured, and the trees are beginning to lose their leaves. Preparations are made for the coming winter. The God is making his exit from the physical plane and heading toward his mythical death at Samhain, and his ultimate rebirth at Yule. Once again, the days and nights are of equal length, symbolizing the temporary nature of all life; no season lasts forever, and neither dark nor light ever overpowers the other for too long. Like the Spring Equinox on the opposite side of the Wheel, the theme here is balance.

The Autumn Equinox is considered in some traditions to be "the Second Harvest," with Lammas being the first and Samhain the last of three harvests. A more recent name for the holiday is Mabon, after a Welsh mythological figure whose origins are connected to a divine "mother and son" pair, echoing the dual nature of the relationship between the Goddess and the God.

≡ SAMHAIN ≡

OCTOBER 31

Considered by many Wiccans to be the most important of the Sabbats, Samhain is the time when death's part in the cycle of life is acknowledged and honored. The word Samhain comes from old Irish and is thought by many to mean "Summer's end." The God in his Sun aspect retreats into the shadows as night begins to dominate the day. As the God of the Hunt, he is a reminder of the sacrifice of life that keeps us alive through the winter months. The harvest is complete and the sacred nature of food is respected. Among some traditions this is viewed as the "Third Harvest."

Wiccan and other Pagan traditions view Samhain as a point on the Wheel when the "veil" between the spiritual and material worlds is at its thinnest, and the days around Samhain are considered especially good for divination activities. Ancestors are honored and communicated with at this time. Many of the Halloween traditions still celebrated in contemporary cultures today can be traced back through the centuries to this festival. Pagans of the old times left food offerings for their ancestors, which eventually evolved into the modern custom of trick-or-treating. Jack-o-lanterns evolved from the practice of leaving candle-lit, hollowed-out root vegetables to guide spirits visiting on Earth.

Some Wiccans in the Celtic traditions consider Samhain, as opposed to Yule, to be the beginning of the year, as the death and rebirth aspects of creation are seen to be inherently joined together—death opens the space for new life to take root. Honoring the ancient Celtic view of the year having a "light half" and a "dark half," their Wheel of the Year begins anew on this day, the first day of the dark half of the year.

THE ESBATS

While the Sabbat celebrations focus on the God and his association with the Sun, the Esbats honor the Goddess in her association with the Moon. Covens traditionally meet on the Esbats for ritual and magic, typically at the Full Moon, although some traditions honor the New Moon instead. They work with the Goddess to bring about healing and assistance for their members and communities, and often work for the good of the wider world as well.

Each Full Moon is seen within the context of the Wheel of the Year, with its own name and seasonal attributions. For Wiccans working with particular aspects of the Goddess, the specific goddess called upon during an Esbat will often correspond with the time of year. For example, Freyja (Norse) is an appropriate goddess to celebrate abundance under a Summer Moon, whereas Persephone (Greek), with her underworld associations, is more appropriate to work with under a late Autumn or early Winter Moon.

The names for each Moon vary from tradition to tradition, but they are generally related to aspects of the season in which they occur. In the Northern Hemisphere, typical Full Moon names are as follows: (*see the chart on the facing page*).

FULL MOON
MONTHS AND NAMES

MONTH	MOON NAME
JANUARY	COLD MOON (also Hunger)
FEBRUARY	QUICKENING MOON (also Snow)
MARCH	STORM MOON (also Sap)
APRIL	WIND MOON (also Pink)
MAY	FLOWER MOON (also Milk)
JUNE	SUN MOON (also Strong Sun and Rose)
JULY	BLESSING MOON (also Thunder)
AUGUST	CORN MOON (also Grain)
SEPTEMBER	HARVEST MOON
OCTOBER	BLOOD MOON
NOVEMBER	MOURNING MOON (also Frost)
DECEMBER	LONG NIGHTS MOON

Many Witches consider astrological influences in addition to seasonal influences and will work according to the particular sign the Moon is in while full. They will refer to the Moon accordingly, such as the "Gemini Moon" or the "Aquarius Moon," and include associations with the Moon's sign in their ritual. When more than one Full Moon occurs in a given calendar month, it's called a Blue Moon. Occurring roughly once every two and a half years, this is considered a particularly powerful time in many Wiccan traditions, and special attention is paid to working with the rare energy of a Blue Moon.

The Elements

One way of connecting with the energies of the natural world and, by extension, the entire Universe, is in relationship with the Elements. The Elements honored in Wiccan rituals may be incorporated in magical work as well.

The recognition of elemental states of matter—Earth, Air, Fire, and Water—has been around since the ancient Greeks, and versions of this concept appear in a number of ancient cultures. In Wicca and other pagan belief systems, the Elements are seen as fundamental aspects of divine energy, each containing qualities that manifest in our personalities and our way of being in the world. In Wiccan practices, each Element is represented in the tangible forms of colors, ritual tools, natural objects, and herbs, as well as the intangible forms of the four cardinal directions, the four seasons, particular deities, and, often, astrological signs.

Working with the Elements can help increase certain desired energies and experiences in our lives, such as love and abundance. Likewise, they can help us balance unwanted experiences rooted in negative qualities, like jealousy or anger.

EARTH

The Earth is the center of our human universe, providing us the foundation of life and keeping us literally grounded through its gravitational pull. It's the source of all plant and animal life, providing us with nourishment and healing. Yet it can also cause physical death and destruction through earthquakes, mudslides and avalanches.

Earth is physically represented by topographical features, such as rocks, soil, caves, fields, forests, and gardens. The Element of Earth is associated with strength, abundance, and prosperity, and is represented by the colors green, yellow, brown, and black. Earth energy is feminine and receptive. Positive qualities associated with Earth are stability, responsibility, respect, and endurance, while negative qualities include stubbornness and rigidity. The Earth's cardinal direction is North, and its season is Winter.

AIR

Air is the invisible Element. Its presence is only seen in the effects it has on other matter—leaves fluttering in the breeze, the movement of the clouds. Although it can't be seen itself, it can be felt all around us, which may be why it's associated with the mind, the intellect, communication, and divination.

It is associated with sky, wind, mountaintops, and birds, and is represented in yellow, white, and silver, among other colors. Air is essential for life as it carries oxygen, and it contributes to abundance by carrying and spreading seeds to new places where they can sprout. It also participates in the destructive force of life with storms and frigid wind. It is a masculine, projective energy. Positive personal qualities associated with Air energy include intelligence, inspiration, and optimism. Negative qualities include gossip and forgetfulness. Air's cardinal direction is East, and its season is Spring.

The awesome, destructive potential of Fire is probably most striking in the seasonal wildfires that burn millions of acres of forest around the world, which can actually jump over rivers and roads to resume their spread on the other side. Lightning can also be deadly, as can extreme heat. Of course, Fire is also life sustaining, and has been used for cooking and lighting for over 100,000 years.

The Element of Fire is associated with the Sun, sunlight, stars, deserts, and volcanoes. It is represented with red, gold, crimson, orange, and white, and is a masculine, projective energy. Fire is the Element of transformation, illumination, health, and strength. Its positive qualities promote love, passion, enthusiasm, courage, and leadership. Negative qualities include hate, jealousy, fear, anger, and conflict. Its season is Summer, and South is its cardinal direction.

WATER

Water is essential for life on Earth and is present in all life. It established forms in the Earth, such as lakes and rivers, by following the path of least resistance, and it can wear away solid rock over time. It is associated with all of its visible physical manifestations, such as streams, springs, oceans, the rain, and the Moon, which exerts its gravitational pull on Water's biggest bodies. Its destructive forces manifest in severe rainstorms, floods, whirlpools, and riptides.

The Element of Water is associated with emotions, healing, dreams, psychic clairvoyance, and the subconscious. Water is receptive and feminine, and is represented by the colors blue, green, indigo, and black. Its positive qualities include compassion, forgiveness, and intuition. Negative qualities are laziness, indifference, insecurity, and lack of control over emotions. Autumn is Water's season, and its cardinal direction is West.

Many Wiccan traditions recognize a Fifth Element that is referred to as Aether, or, more commonly, Spirit.

This is the Element present in all things, immaterial but essential for connection and balance between all other Elements. It has been described as the binding force through which manifestation is made possible, as well as the divine intelligence of the "All" that spiritualists of many traditions seek connection with. The Fifth Element, also known as Akasha, from the Sanskrit word for *aether*, is found in Buddhism, Hinduism, and other religions, and is translated by some as "inner space" or "open space."

The Fifth Element is represented by the color white. Unlike the other Elements, it has no gender, energy type, or cardinal direction. It has no season; rather, it is associated with the entire Wheel of the Year.

OTHER BELIEFS

BORROWING AS IT DOES FROM MANY OLDER SPIRITUAL traditions, Wicca is inherently a "patchwork" system of beliefs. In addition to what has already been discussed, other beliefs commonly found among Wiccans include reincarnation, animism, the Elements that make up all of Nature, and astrological and numerological traditions.

Reincarnation

The idea that we live many different lifetimes is found in several religions, including Hinduism, Buddhism, and Jainism, as well as in other ancient and modern cultures.

Wicca has adopted this belief in various ways, which differ from coven to coven and individual to individual. While some believe that we can and sometimes do choose to reincarnate in non-human forms, i.e. as animals or plants, many others believe that we only come back as humans.

Either way, reincarnation is seen as a logical extension of the life/death/rebirth cycle observed in the natural world and celebrated throughout the Wheel of the Year. It can also be used as a lens through which to look at life struggles as soul lessons, giving meaning to each of the challenges we experience.

While it's not currently possible to verify the existence of past lives in a scientific manner, many Wiccans and other spiritual seekers perceive at least some details of a past before this life, while others may have a sense of having "been here" before. This feeling may occur in or near a place where a past life was lived, or manifest as an affinity for a particular time period in history or a country or continent that one has never visited in this lifetime. A common "past life history" among Witches involves at least one prior life as a Witch, often one that ended in some form of persecution. Many of these Witches feel they have chosen to come back now in order to practice their Craft in an atmosphere of freedom and religious tolerance.

Wiccans and spiritual healers of many traditions today employ meditation, past-life regression, and dream analysis techniques to help people recall their past lives as a way of understanding their current problems. It is thought that whatever spiritual lessons were not learned in the past can be actively worked on in this life, a belief that stirs the soul to learn new lessons, both in this and future lives.

The Afterlife

Wiccans generally believe in an afterlife of some form or another, but not one that resembles the Christian concepts of heaven or hell. Names and descriptions for this realm vary widely and may be based on older pagan belief systems or be more idiosyncratic. Common names include the Otherworld, the Afterworld, Summerland, and the Shining Land, among others. Some describe it as a naturally abundant and beautiful place, while others see it more as an entity that doesn't resemble any physical reality on Earth.

Ultimately each individual's experience and perception will inform their notion of what's beyond that which we can physically perceive as this life. Those who believe in reincarnation will say that this is the place where our souls spend time between incarnations, rather than a final destination. Some believe it's a place to make choices about our next incarnations based on what we've learned, or haven't yet learned, so far, on our soul's journey.

Animism

As mentioned earlier, Wicca is essentially a form of animism. In the most basic sense, animism is the belief that everything in the material world has a "soul" or a "spirit." This applies to all non-human animals as well as the geographical and ecological phenomena of mountains, rivers, trees, and anything else found on Earth. Many indigenous cultures operate from an animistic perspective, including several Native American belief systems and the traditional Japanese Shinto religion.

Animism provides a way of seeing into the divine relationship between humans and the natural world, as particular stones, trees, and streams may be imbued with a special sense of energy and held as sacred sites of worship. The Celtic belief in fairies (also spelled *faeries*) can be seen as a form of animism, as they are themselves generally invisible but thought to live in hills, mounds, woodlands, and other natural phenomena. Many other pagan cultures acknowledged the presence of "Elemental spirits" as well, such as gnomes, elves, sylphs, and the like.

For some, animism also powers the workings of magic, as objects used in ritual are believed to possess their own spirit energies, and are joined with those of the Witch to create the change being sought. The spirits of the surrounding land and/or the Elemental beings may also be asked for assistance in ritual and magic.

Stars, Numbers, Tarot, and More

As mentioned earlier, Wicca's founding was influenced in large part by other occult philosophies and ancient belief systems within the Western Mystery Tradition. As such, there is a lot of overlap between these influences and what we now think of as Wicca. While not all Wiccans incorporate everything described here into their practice, many do work with one or more of these occult systems.

The ancient traditions of astrology provide a way to view events on Earth in the context of the energies and locations of celestial bodies. Astrological systems vary from culture to culture, but Wicca tends to incorporate Western astrology with its focus on the Sun, the Moon, and the planets of our Solar System.

The signs of the Zodiac wheel, which measure the Sun's path across the celestial sphere according to how it looks from Earth, are named for constellations and assigned "ruling" planets that influence behavior and phenomena in particular ways.

The horoscopes that most people are familiar with today represent only a fraction of the information contained in astrology, as they tend to focus solely on a person's Sun sign. The full picture of a person's personality makeup and potential life paths is much more complex. Many Wiccans know at least the basics of their astrological birth charts—their Sun sign, Moon sign and Rising sign—as well as the general "personality type" of each sign in the Zodiac wheel.

The current position of both the Sun and Moon at any given time is often taken into consideration when working magic for a particular purpose. The Moon's current sign is especially important for Esbats, with different signs being more or less favorable for specific intentions. Witches who are more knowledgeable about astrology may also work with additional aspects, such as the current positions of other planets.

Numerology delves into the spiritual and/or magical energies of numbers. Everyone has their own set of significant numbers, based on their birth date and the letters in their name (each letter of the alphabet is assigned a number between 1 and 9). Each number has its own energy and characteristics that manifest as personality traits and life experiences.

Numerological significances can be incorporated into Wiccan practice in ritual, magic, and divination methods. The number 3 is particularly significant to Wiccans, as seen in the three aspects of the Triple Goddess. Some practitioners choose a sacred "Wiccan name" for themselves based on numerological systems.

Finally, different methods and traditions of divination are often part of Wiccan practice. Witches use Tarot cards, pendulums, runes, the Celtic Ogham, and objects for "scrying" (such as crystal balls, mirrors, and the surface of still water) to communicate with unseen energies and discover the hidden forces at work in their unfolding lives.

Witches might consult their preferred divination tools for insight into how best to set their intentions for a coming ritual. Divination may also be part of ritual or occur immediately after, but can be practiced at any time. Astrology and numerology are often intertwined with these practices, especially in Tarot and other forms of divination cards.

PART TWO

WICCAN
RITUAL

FROM BELIEF TO PRACTICE

NOW THAT WE'VE TAKEN A BRIEF LOOK AT THE ORIGINS AND the basic belief systems of modern Wicca, let's take a closer look at how these belief systems are enacted through religious ritual.

In part two, we'll explore the inspirations for and philosophy behind Wiccan ritual and outline the basic components of a typical Wiccan celebration. You'll also find a comprehensive overview of the tools used in ritual, including their associated symbolism, their purposes, and how you can acquire tools of very own.

COMMUNING WITH THE DIVINE

WHILE WICCA IS ULTIMATELY A SPIRITUAL PATH WITH relevance to every aspect of one's life, many Wiccans consider the ritual experience to be the heart of their practice. Ritual is a purposeful, focused communion with the energies underlying all of creation. At each Sabbat and Esbat, covens and circles gather to honor the Goddess and God and celebrate the wonders to be found in the ongoing cycles of life. The rituals of solitary Wiccans are no less significant, as each person tapping into this Universal energy is adding their personal light and power to the collective at these special times.

Depending on the tradition, rituals can take various forms, with no two occasions being exactly alike. Formats may differ, depending on whether the ritual is a Sabbat, an Esbat, or a milestone ritual, such as a handfasting (wedding), an initiation, or an end-of-life ceremony. Coven rituals tend to be more highly structured and elaborate than those of circles and solitaries, although anyone following an established tradition might practice in a more formalized manner than many eclectic Wiccans. Since most covens keep the details of their rituals secret, and are known only to initiated members, it's difficult to describe them here with much accuracy. However, the basic "bones" of a typical ritual are widely known and will be described in this section.

Wiccan Ritual and Ceremonial Magic

As mentioned in part one, the practices of what we know now as Wicca were inspired by a variety of occult influences within the Western Mystery Tradition, as well as the practices of secret societies like the Freemasons and the Hermetic Order of the Golden Dawn. These groups were influenced by older medieval occult texts, many of which were themselves rooted in even older traditions and practices. One significant influence in particular, for Gerald Gardner, was the practice of ceremonial magic, also known as "high magic," the purpose of which is to interact directly with the spirit world. Using specific ritual actions and words, practitioners of high magic are able to summon or invoke spirits, deities, and other non-physical entities.

It's important to note here that these activities aren't always to one's benefit and should not be undertaken without proper study and precaution. The non-physical world is full of all kinds of unpleasant entities, many of which are happy to take any invitation to come in and influence your own personal energy. Protection is very important, in practices like these, in order to keep out entities or other energies you don't want interfering with your experience, whether it be in ritual, spellwork, or just going about your daily life. Fortunately, Wiccan rituals have built-in components that protect practitioners from unwanted energy—namely, the casting of the sacred circle, which will be discussed on pages 61–64.

Furthermore, although some in the Wiccan community don't like to acknowledge it, not everyone who uses ceremonial magic does it for positive purposes. Throughout history, people have used their knowledge of practices like these to influence others and/or events to serve their own interests, and even to cause serious harm. It's important to recognize that magic in and of itself is inherently neutral. It is the intention of the practitioner that makes any magical working positive, neutral, or negative.

In Wiccan practice the purpose of ritual words and actions is to commune with the divine Universe, via the energies of the Elements and the Goddess and God. This is done through movement, words, and special ritual tools in a focused manner that aligns the energy of the practitioner with the higher realms. Essentially, the ritual space facilitates an altered state of consciousness not unlike those utilized by traditional shamanic cultures. Within the sacred circle, the mundane concerns of life fade away and higher-level energetic vibrations are easily perceived. This is where the most intense and personal connections with the God and Goddess are experienced.

The act of creating and strengthening this sacred space is often referred to as "raising energy." Energy is all around us, of course, but it can be intentionally shaped and directed, as is demonstrated by Tai Chi, Reiki, and other spiritual healing practices. In Wiccan ritual, this energy is channeled into specific purposes, such as appreciation and gratitude for one's blessings, requests for assistance from the spirit world, and intentions for healing the planet. The energy also forms bonds between the ritual participants, particularly among coven members.

Again, the form any given ritual takes will depend on the tradition being followed and the ritual occasion. That being said, there are a few common components that typically follow the same order: a sacred circle is cast, the Elements and Wiccan deities are invoked, and food and drink are shared with the deities and among the participants. The ritual then ends with the closing of the circle. Movement, dance, chanting, singing, spoken prayers, and/or spellwork may also be part of the activities. The Wiccan altar, laid out with various ritual tools in a specific order, is always the focal point of the ritual.

We'll discuss the altar and the core components of a "standard" ritual in greater detail over the following pages. You'll also find an overview of the various tools used in Wiccan ritual, describing the significance and function of each, along with some suggestions on how to acquire them. By the end of this section, you will be prepared to begin building your own ritual practice.

THE WICCAN ALTAR

SINCE ANCIENT TIMES, CULTURES AROUND THE WORLD HAVE employed the use of an altar for the purposes of worship, prayer, and magical activity, such as divination or spellcasting. We see evidence of this in the ancient cultures of Greece, Rome, Norway, Egypt, and Ireland (just to name a handful), where altars were used to venerate deities, leave offerings, make sacrifices, and send prayers. Many deities, beliefs, and folk traditions from these cultures have come to influence modern Wicca.

As with any other religion or spiritual tradition, the altar in Wicca is a place to both worship and connect with the divine. However, unlike many other religions, Wicca provides an avenue for a very direct kind of participation—what we might actually call "co-creation" with the forces of the Universe that shape our daily lives. Through meditation, energy raising, prayer, and/or spell-work, Wiccans work actively to improve the state of things in their personal spheres as well as in the world at large. The altar serves as the physical focal point for this work. It is chiefly used for ritual celebrations of the eight Sabbats and thirteen Esbats, but can also be used at any other time, such as during spellwork, meditation, or prayer.

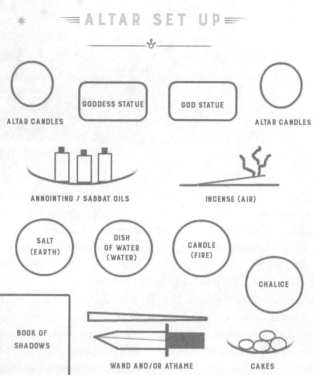

ALTAR CANDLES

GODDESS STATUE

GOD STATUE

ALTAR CANDLES

ANNOINTING / SABBAT OILS

INCENSE (AIR)

SALT
(EARTH)

DISH
OF WATER
(WATER)

CANDLE
(FIRE)

CHALICE

BOOK OF
SHADOWS

WAND AND/OR ATHAME

CAKES

Traditionally, the altar stands in the center of the circle of sacred energy created by the participant(s) in the ritual. The tools are deliberately placed in specific places on the altar that correspond with the particular energies of the God and Goddess, the Elements, and the four cardinal directions. For example, tools and symbols associated with the element of Earth may be placed in the North section of the altar, while those associated with water are placed to the West. In Traditional Wicca, the altar is laid out in a fairly elaborate manner, with several ritual tools in very specific places. Typically, the left side of the altar corresponds to the Goddess, meaning that the tools placed to the left will be related to the Goddess in some way, while the right side corresponds to the God. The altar is traditionally positioned to face either the East or the North point of the circle but may also face the cardinal direction that corresponds with the Witch's dominant element. For example, if you have a lot of Water in your astrological chart, you might use a West-facing altar. Covens performing group rituals will generally have a standard arrangement for their altar, based on the particular tradition that they follow, although more eclectic covens might create their own traditional arrangement.

The same is true for solitary Wiccans—many closely follow established patterns for setting up the altar; others experiment and use patterns that resonate with their personal practice. They may or may not incorporate every single tool used in Traditional Wicca. Those with small altars and limited space may be quite economical in their approach, preferring just three or four objects. Some people like to keep the center of the altar completely clear in order to focus more intently on spellwork or perform divination with runes.

A traditionally based layout you can try and/or modify according to your intuition is shown on the opposite page.

What Do "Tools" Have to Do with It?

Some newcomers may find "tools" to be a rather odd word choice to use in a spiritual or religious context. Typically, this term isn't used outside of ceremonial magic and various forms of Witchcraft. But the word "tools" underscores the Wiccan belief that we are not just passive recipients of the benevolent energy of the Universe— we also actively work to engage with and even shape it.

Each tool is a unique and powerful representation of an aspect of Universal energy, whether through its alignment with an Element, the God and/or Goddess, or another personal deity. But the tools are essentially both symbolic *and* practical. As physical objects, they assist with harnessing and directing magical energies in the spiritual (or nonphysical) realms, according to our intent.

Tools are always cleared of residual energy, when first acquired, and later consecrated for ritual use. Wiccans know that everything on Earth is made of energy, and interactions between people and inanimate objects can leave energetic imprints on both. For example, if your ritual candles were handled by a disgruntled retail worker having a very bad day, the energy of frustration or despair is likely to linger on the candles. Once this unwanted energy is cleared away, the tool is then consecrated (or dedicated) to the purpose of honoring the Goddess and God and communing with divine energy.

All this being said, the truth is that tools are not really strictly necessary—adept Wiccans and other Witches can work with sacred energy without them, simply by drawing on their personal power and focused attention. But, as sensory creatures who learn from symbols and patterns, the use of tools is a great help in training and keeping our focus where it needs to be—in the energetically charged space of the sacred circle. And since the vast majority of Wiccans use these tools, we are joining up with the collective power of their energetic influence on the spiritual plane when we do so.

Don't worry if the use of ritual tools doesn't make a lot of sense right away—this can be one of the trickier aspects of Wicca to grasp. This is one of many reasons why it's recommended to do a lot of studying before devoting yourself to the practice of Wicca. In fact, there's a tradition of studying for a year and a day before making any serious commitment to either a coven or a solitary practice.

CORE COMPONENTS OF
WICCAN RITUAL

ALTHOUGH THE EXACT PROCEEDING OF A GIVEN RITUAL WILL depend on the occasion and the tradition or style of the practitioner(s), there is an established framework for beginning Wiccans to follow. One of the most important steps, however, actually begins before the ritual itself—that of purification.

Both the space where the proceedings are to be held as well as the personal energy field of the celebrant(s) should be ritually purified of any negative or otherwise unwanted energetic influence. The ritual space can be smudged with purifying herbs like sage or rosemary, or aspersed (sprinkled) with water that has been blessed for the purpose. The besom, or sacred broom, may also be used to disperse unwanted energy. The participant(s) in the ritual also purify themselves with a ritual bath and/or smudging. Once the energy field of both the Witch and the space is clear, the ritual can begin.

Casting the Sacred Circle

Traditionally, every ritual and every magical working begins by establishing an energetic perimeter around the participant(s). This practice also comes from ceremonial magic, where it is chiefly used as a means of protection from undesirable energy and nonphysical entities. The Wiccan circle also protects, but its chief purpose is to create a physical space where divine energy is concentrated and amplified. Divine energy is everywhere all the time, of course, but it often escapes our perception in everyday life.

In Traditional Wicca, the circle extends upward, far above the group, and tapers toward the top to form what Gardner called the Cone of Power. (Perhaps this is where the phrase "raising energy" comes from.) Many solitary practitioners may perform a solo version of this method but creating the Cone of Power isn't strictly necessary to ritual.

As a symbol, the circle represents the Moon, the Earth, and the abundance of the Goddess. For this reason a circle is able to safely contain the physical quantity of energy raised by the Witch or Witches performing the ritual and see its transformation through to the higher realms. The circle is an infinitely portable tool, as it can be drawn anywhere, either physically or psychically, or subtly or elaborately, depending on the circumstances. The circle may be as big or small as appropriate, but it must have enough room for the altar, everything being used in the ritual, and everyone participating.

You can imagine the circle as a force field that keeps negativity and the mundane "noise" of everyday life from affecting the energy of your sacred space. Woven with your energy and the energy of the five elements of Earth, Air, Fire, Water, and Akasha (spirit), the circle is a powerful vortex where time can seemingly stand still, when you are within it. It is a protective bubble that can be likened to the walls of a church, mosque, or synagogue—whatever is going on outside of the circle is sealed off. This "force field" isn't always very noticeable to beginners, especially those working alone, but with practice the energy becomes more palpable, until the difference between being in the circle and being in ordinary reality is very obvious.

The circle is considered sacred ground from the moment it is drawn until it is closed at the end of the ritual. Once energy is raised inside the circle, the circle must remain closed. No one can step outside of the circle while it is active without first performing an energetic manipulation, such as a "circle-cutting" spell, which creates an energetic "doorway," safe enough to exit and re-enter without disturbing the circle's energy. Once the circle is re-entered, the doorway is closed.

Marking the Circle

The circle is usually marked on the floor of the space being used for ritual, often with sea salt first, followed by candles to mark the four cardinal directions. Each direction corresponds to a specific element: east for Air, south for Fire, west for Water, and north for Earth. Larger areas can accommodate pillar candles, and tiki torches work well outside. If you are in your bedroom, you may want to invest in a few inexpensive battery-operated tea lights or real tea lights in enclosed lanterns that cannot easily overturn and singe robes or long skirts.

If using fire is unworkable for whatever reason, you can use other magical items that are charged with energy for the purpose of ritual, such as crystals and semiprecious gemstones, or even herbs. These items can be chosen according to their correspondences—for example, malachite and tiger's eye are both associated with Earth, and so would be placed in the North.

Some like to further mark the circle with sea salt, pebbles, or a long piece of cord kept for this purpose. Others may simply visualize the circle filling in with white light. The circle can also be "drawn" with a wand or athame, or even one's pointer finger. This may be done from the center of the circle, or while walking the circle, just inside its boundaries. Casting a circle is always done traveling deosil, or clockwise, typically beginning at due East. (However, some Wiccans like to begin with the direction that corresponds with their ruling element, so if you're a water sign, for example, you would start with the West.)

Calling the Quarters and Invoking the Deities

Not everyone draws the circle—some merely mark the quarters and then begin with the step of "calling," or invoking, the Quarters. The Quarters are a name for the energies of the four Elements and their respective cardinal directions. They are also known as the Guardians of the Watchtowers or, more simply, the Watchtowers. Borrowed from ceremonial magic, this ritual brings in both the protective and co-creative energies of Nature and serves to complete the work of casting the circle before the heart of the Sabbat, Esbat, or other celebration begins.

Calling the Quarters can take a variety of forms. In a coven, for example, the High Priestess, High Priest, or a coven member may walk around the circle, stopping in each cardinal direction to invoke the presence of its associated Element, using specific words and/or gestures. (It should be remembered here that not all coven structures involve hierarchy—in some covens each member simply takes a turn to perform this and any other necessary roles in ritual.)

In more elaborate versions, each Quarter is invoked with a corresponding ritual tool that aligns with the direction's element. For example, if starting with the East, incense may be carried as a representation of the Element of Air. (These correspondences are covered in the ritual tool descriptions on pages 69–89.)

These days, eclectic Wiccans often take a more pared-down approach. A solitary Witch may simply stand at the altar, perhaps with a wand, and turn to face each direction while invoking its associated Element. In many traditions, the fifth Element—Akasha, or Spirit—is called in after the four Quarters. Those just starting out may follow a specific version of this ritual from a book or other source and experiment with different approaches (or invent a method of their own), before finding the one that works best for them.

After the Quarters are called, the next step is to invoke the Goddess and the God and invite them to be present throughout the ritual. This can take many different forms, but usually involves words of some kind, which may or may not be in poetic verse. Appropriate ritual tools may also be raised to greet the deities. For solitaries, this aspect of ritual can be intensely personal, and beginners may need to try various approaches, as they learn to inhabit their own sacred space. The main thing to know is that the God and Goddess are always present, as they are present in each living and nonliving thing in the Universe. They are not far from anyone wishing to connect with them. We simply have to learn how to attune to their presence.

The Heart of Ritual and the Book of Shadows

Once the circle is cast, the Quarters are called, and the God and Goddess are invoked, the sacred space is ready for the heart of the ritual, depending on the occasion. If it's a Sabbat celebration, there may be a focus on the turning of the Wheel of the Year with special words, songs, or other content related to the seasonal theme of the Sabbat. An Esbat may focus on the sacred energies of the Goddess and include petitions for assistance with healing an illness or needs on the part of the practitioner(s), or even the entire planet. Milestone rituals, such as a handfasting or an initiation rite, may have their own special content related to the purpose.

Many coven rituals include a dramatic performance—such as re-enacting scenes from ancient myths or poems—or other liturgical material. Solitary Wiccans might also read passages from ancient mystic texts or compose their own poetry or stories for the occasion. Dancing and/or other ritual gestures may also be part of the proceedings. Spellwork may also occur at this time, although many Wiccans prefer to keep their magical practice separate from Sabbat celebrations, reserving Esbats or other moments unrelated to the Wheel of the Year for this purpose. Divination may also be employed, particularly at Samhain, although it might take place after the ritual as well.

Traditionally, the words, format, and other instructions for rituals of all kinds are kept in the coven's (or solitary's) Book of Shadows. The term "Book of Shadows" comes out of the Gardnerian Tradition, but has been widely adopted and adapted by covens, solitaries, and eclectics ever since. It is a type of *grimoire*—or book of rituals, spells and/or magical lore that is intended for the practitioner's eyes only. The contents of a Book of Shadows vary from Witch to Witch or coven to coven. In Traditional Wicca, much of this information would have been handed down from prior generations, some of it going all the way back to Gardner's day.

Keeping a Book of Shadows is a great way for new and experienced Witches alike to deepen their practice of the Craft. In addition to recording ritual material, some may also record the results of their magical workings, information about their personal deity alignments, or lists of herbs and stones for which they feel with a particular affinity. A Book of Shadows can also be a good place to record relevant dreams—or other signs and messages that come into your life—and free-write about your intentions for a coming ritual or a new season. You can think of your Book of Shadows as a kind of journal, specifically for spiritual and/or magical pursuits.

Basically, any information you find to be important or helpful as you progress along your path is worth recording.

Cakes and Ale

After the main work of the ritual is completed, a ceremony known variously as "cakes and ale," "cakes and wine," or "bread and wine" takes place. Food and drink are offered to the Goddess and God, and then shared among the ritual participants. This ceremony obviously has parallels with similar rituals in other religions, like communion in Christianity and the blessing of the Shabbat bread and wine in Judaism, showing that the sharing of food and drink can be a very sacred act.

"Cakes and ale" is an old English phrase meaning "the good things in life." This is a moment to appreciate the ever-present love of the Goddess and God and any blessings you feel particularly thankful for at this time. There are several versions of this ceremony, and the actual food and beverage used may differ across traditions and eclectic practices. Generally speaking, the "ale," which can also be wine, water, or juice, is poured in the chalice, which is then lifted up to the God and Goddess before it is sipped by the practitioner(s). In coven rituals, the chalice may be passed from Witch to Witch, each of whom takes a sip from the ritual drink. The cakes, bread, or other food may then be passed around the circle for all to share.

The ceremony of cakes and ale serves two main purposes. The first is to honor and thank the deities for attending the ritual and being present in your life in general. The second is to help practitioners "ground" their personal energy after what is often an intense ritual experience. The words spoken during this ceremony may be scripted in the Book of Shadows, or may be more informal, but many versions of cakes and ale include the phrases "may you never hunger" and "may you never thirst" when passing the ritual food and drink around the circle. (Solitaries may change these phrases to "may I never hunger" and "may I never thirst" before partaking.)

Closing the Ritual

Once all of the ritual work is completed, it's time to formally "close," or dissolve, the sacred circle. This step ensures that the energy raised during ritual has gone completely to its destination in the higher realms and is not squandered or neglected on the physical plane. It also helps ground the participant(s) more firmly in the physical plane after reaching intense states of consciousness. (If you've ever been abruptly pulled out of a deep meditative state, you'll understand the importance of closing the ritual in an appropriate manner!)

Typically, the ritual is closed in a reverse manner to the way it was initiated. First, the God and Goddess are thanked for their presence and participation. Then the Quarters are thanked and "released" or "dismissed." The circle is walked in the widdershins (or counterclockwise) direction, beginning at the same cardinal point where the casting started. Quarter-markers and anything else used to mark the circumference of the circle is retrieved or swept away. You may also wish to disperse any excess energy with a ritual broom, a smudge stick, or even just your hands.

After the ritual, covens may enjoy a feast or other social time. Solitary Witches might spend some time in meditation, go for a nice walk, or do something else that allows them to bask in the positive vibrations of the ritual experience.

THE TOOLS OF
WICCAN RITUAL

A S WE HAVE SEEN, WICCANS INCORPORATE A VARIETY OF objects into their ritual and magical practices. Some of these are familiar to mainstream culture, although they are usually misunderstood. Magic powers don't come streaming in a bolt of light from a Witch's wand, and no one literally flies on a broom. Both tools are important and sacred to Witchcraft, but the way they are used, and their effects on the world at large, are much more subtle.

In reality, a Witch might not use a wand or a broom in their personal practice. Traditions vary widely in terms of which tools are considered essential to ritual work. Many of the tools used most commonly are borrowed from ceremonial magic—chiefly, the wand, the athame, the pentacle, and the chalice. Other tools come from older folk magic symbology, typically from pagan traditions of European origin. For example, the cauldron is significant in Celtic mythology and incense has been a part of religious activity since before recorded history. The wand, as it happens, is actually a shortened version of the staff, which has been used in religious and magical contexts in many ancient cultures.

It's important to remember that the power involved in Witchcraft is harnessed by Witches themselves—the tools are merely assistants. They can be charged with magical energy, and they may be very near and dear to the Witch, but they still need the energy of the Witch's intention, or will, in order to work.

The following pages provide an introduction to the tools of Wiccan ritual. You'll find information here about the symbolic significance of each tool, its main ritual purpose(s), and how you might go about acquiring (or making) these tools for your own practice.

CORE RITUAL TOOLS

THE FOLLOWING ITEMS ARE THE MOST WIDELY ACKNOWLEDGED as the "core tools" of ritual, although even this list varies among traditions and even more so among eclectic solitary practitioners. For example, some Wiccans might not use a wand at all, while others might forego the athame but consider the bell to be essential.

As you read about these tools, pay attention to any intuitive responses to certain items. If you feel energized by reading about a specific tool, that's a good one to start with as you begin building your ritual practice.

The Altar

Firstly, you'll need an altar. (At a minimum, you'll need a special cloth to lay out on the floor if a physical altar isn't possible just yet.) The altar is often a table or other object with a flat surface, such as an old chest or a nightstand. It can be square or round, according to preference. Ideally, the altar is made of wood, such as oak, which is considered to hold significant power, or willow, which is known to be sacred to the Goddess.

Witches performing outdoor rituals may use an old tree stump, large stone, or other natural object for an altar, or use a fire as the focal point, placing the ritual tools elsewhere in the charged space. In general, natural materials like wood, stone, and marble are always favored over synthetic materials like vinyl or Formica, but in truth, any physical object charged with magical energy will contribute power to the ritual work being enacted.

While the altar is usually set up prior to the ritual and taken down afterward, some practitioners maintain permanent altars in their homes. These may double as shrines to the Goddess and God and can be a place to store the Witch's magical tools. However, plenty of Wiccans don't have space for a permanent altar.

Sometimes kitchen and coffee tables are temporarily "repurposed" for Sabbats, Esbats, and spellwork. Witches often decorate the altar with colored scarves or other fabric, corresponding with the season or with the particular ritual occasion. Doing so helps transform an ordinary piece of furniture into a sacred object for the duration of the ritual.

Use what you have on hand or can find in a second-hand furniture store. With a little imagination, you might be able to permanently repurpose a modest-sized trunk or chest of drawers, using the interior to store your magical tools, while not drawing unwanted attention to the altar from visitors or family members, if you're not open about your Wiccan practice.

Deity Representations

For many Wiccans, deity representations are probably the most important objects on the altar. Typically, these take the form of either designated candles, possibly carved with symbols associated with the God and Goddess, or visual images, such as sculptures or drawings. Those whose practices are rooted in Gardnerian Wicca may follow the tradition of using a silver candle to represent the Goddess and a gold candle for the God, although some traditions use a white or green candle for the Goddess and a red or yellow candle for the God.

Those who work with specific goddesses and gods (generally viewed within Wicca as "aspects" of the supreme Goddess and God) often use visual images of the deity. For example, followers of the Norse pantheon may represent Freyja and Odin with sculptures in their likeness, while those working within a Celtic tradition might use engravings or paintings of Brigh and the Dagda. Polytheists, who work with one or more additional deities (often referred to as "patron" deities), may also include a representation for each on their altar.

Other traditions, particularly those within Dianic Wicca, place a great deal of emphasis on the power of the Goddess, and may use a single representation of the divine on their altars, in the form of their ancient patron goddess or the Wiccan Triple Goddess.

Note that you don't *have* to use visual images of any deities with whom you choose to work. You can always represent them with a candle in a color that is associated with them or another symbol that you recognize as representing them.

Candles

While not exactly the most mysterious or obscure ritual tool, candles are widely considered essential to the practice of Wicca. Perhaps this is due to their literal embodiment of the Element of Fire. Whatever the case, many would agree that even candles used in the most mundane of contexts seem to have a magical way about them.

Witches work with a variety of candle shapes, sizes, and colors, depending on the candle's purpose. Color choices may correspond with the deities being represented and/or invoked, the Sabbat being celebrated, or the particular magical purpose of a ritual or spell. (Candles used in spellwork are discussed in part three, page 124.)

Altar candles (also known as "illuminator" candles) provide general lighting for your working surface during ritual. Tall pillar candles work well for this purpose, as they are long lasting and don't drip wax. You can also use taper candles, which are somewhat more elegant. These can be unwieldy, however, and potentially much messier, so you'll probably want candleholders that will keep the dripping wax from getting on the altar.

You'll want at least two or more illuminator candles (depending on the size of your workspace) to sit off to the sides, at the top corners of the altar. These candles are typically black, a color that lends protection against negativity, and/or white, which symbolizes purity and the Element of Spirit, or Akasha.

As discussed earlier, candles may be used to mark the circle, and are also used to represent the God and Goddess on the altar. Many Wiccans also use a candle to represent the Element of Fire (explained on page 75).

Candles used in the Craft do not need to be fancy or expensive, although there are some beautiful and well-made candles of all sizes to be found in Wiccan supply shops. If you can afford them, soy or beeswax candles are cleaner burning and more environmentally friendly than cheaper paraffin wax alternatives. The main thing is to avoid artificially scented candles, which distract from the work, rather than enhancing it.

If you already light one or more candles regularly, simply to enhance your living space, you can use some of them to illuminate the room you're working in during ritual. However, most Witches distinguish these "mundane" candles from those used within the circle. Candles consecrated for ritual and/or magical use are therefore not used for any other purposes.

Elemental Representations

As we saw earlier, the Elements—Earth, Air, Fire, Water, and Spirit—are integral aspects of Wiccan belief and therefore a key part of ritual. The Elements are invited to participate in the ritual and lend their specific energies to the work. They are also physically represented on the altar with ritual tools and other items.

Every ritual tool has an Elemental association, and in some traditions, these tools may do "double duty" as Elemental representations. For example, although the chalice serves the function of offering libations to the Goddess and God, it may also be considered the representation of Water, especially if it has already been used to welcome in this Element. Many traditions, however, include an additional bowl of water on the altar for the sole purpose of representing and honoring this Element. The main thing is to have at least one object representing each Element to balance the energy of your altar. Here are some items you might possibly use:

EARTH is typically represented by a small dish of soil, sand, sea salt, or even small pebbles (which are especially nice to use in outdoor rituals). Ideally, the dish holding your Earth representation should be used for this purpose only and kept with your ritual items rather than in a kitchen cabinet. You might also use a nice round stone, or even a small plant, depending on the size of your altar.

AIR is traditionally represented by incense, which can be considered a "double duty" tool since it serves other functions as well. (More on incense on pages 83–87.) However, a feather, a bell, small wind chimes, or even a leaf that has been blown off a tree by the wind can also represent Air.

FIRE is among the easier Elements to represent, in a very literal way, with a candle dedicated specifically to this purpose. Choose a color that's associated with Fire—any shade of red or orange is lovely—and if you like, anoint it with an essential oil that corresponds with this Element. You can use a pillar, votive, taper, or even a small spell candle, depending on the size of your altar. If yet another candle on your altar isn't practical, you can also use crystals associated with Fire (typically anything orange or red), a cinnamon stick, or a dried hot chili pepper, if need be.

WATER is also typically represented, quite literally, in a small bowl that sits with the other Elemental representations. The water can be charged with the energy of the Moon or Sun, or even the energies of certain crystals, but "plain old" water will do just fine. This water is not for drinking—it will be picking up a lot of different energies (and perhaps an accidental bit of herb, oil, or wax now and again), so it's best not to ingest it. Your Water dish can be as plain or ornate as you like, but as with the Earth dish, keep it with your other altar tools. A seashell, a piece of driftwood, a small mirror, a moonstone, or a wand of selenite can also represent water.

As you can see, there are options for getting creative with Elemental representations. While it's helpful to follow tradition here, those with smaller altars may need to scale it down a bit. One possibility is to use a crystal associated with each Element or an herb bundle containing one herb for each of the Elements. This can be a great strategy for rituals on the fly—when traveling, for example—and is a good way to start learning about the energetic properties of crystals and herbs.

Wand

Used for millennia in religious and magical rites, the wand has long been associated with Witches and Witchcraft in popular culture, and like its fellow symbol, the broom, it has been quite misunderstood. As with all magical tools, it is not the wand that causes magical transformation, but the Witch, who energetically charges the wand with magical intention. Its linear form makes it an excellent tool for directing energy in ritual. The wand is often used to draw the circle and invoke the Goddess and God and may be used to draw magical symbols in the air or on the ground. Considered sacred to the God, the wand is associated with the Element of Air, in some traditions, and the Element of Fire in others.

Wands can be made of nearly any material, but the general esthetic in Wicca is an emphasis on the Earth as the origin of all tools. Therefore, wands are typically made from wood, crystal, and/or metal. If you want to treat yourself to one of these lovely wands as a way of beginning your practice, you can find a wide variety of beautiful handcrafted wands online and in magical supply shops. These range from lengths of pewter or glass with crystal points fastened to their ends; to more rustic versions made of wood, with carvings and perhaps leather braiding; to a simple skinny length of tumbled gemstone.

It's worth noting, however, that a wand made by the Witch who uses it is generally thought to be more effective. A great way to acquire a wand that's meant just for you is to venture out into the woods! Move through the trees until you come across a nice branch or twig that has already fallen to the ground. (Typically, the wand isn't much longer than the forearm, and can be shorter. In fact, anything that's more than 12 inches (30.5 cm) in length isn't going to be very practical.) Woods traditionally used to make the wand include oak, willow, elder, and hazel, but any tree that grows near you will work.

Some Witches prefer to work with a branch cut from a live tree. This should be done carefully and with an attitude of reverence and respect for the tree. Cutting branches can leave the tree exposed to harmful mold and bacteria, so if you go this route, avoid harvesting your wand in damp weather. Be sure to cut the branch as close to the base as possible and use a white-handled knife known as a *boline* (see page 126) or other sharp knife, rather than garden shears.

When you find a tree that speaks specifically to you, ask permission from the tree to take the branch for your work. Take note of how you feel physically in the moment. If you sense that permission has been granted, gently cut the branch and leave an offering for the tree in thanks.

The branch is then yours to decorate as you please. There are some great DIY projects online for adding a crystal point to the wand, carving magical symbols into it, or wrapping it in tooled leather. If harvesting a branch from a tree isn't possible, you might also purchase a wooden dowel from a craft or hardware store to decorate and consecrate as a wand.

Pentacle

In Wiccan practice, "pentacle" has a couple of different meanings. In general terms, the pentacle is a flat, circular slab made of stone, silver, wood, clay, or wax, on which one or magical symbols is inscribed. The most common symbol found on this tool is also known as a pentacle, a five-pointed star, drawn with five straight lines of equal length, surrounded by a circle. Each point is said to represent the Elements of Air, Earth, Fire, and Water, with the Fifth Element (Spirit) as the upward point. In this sense, it stands for the interconnectedness of all things, including the connection between our own personal energy with that of the Universe.

The pentacle doesn't belong to Wicca alone, of course. As an ancient symbol, going back to at least sixth century BCE, it is found in both ancient Eastern and Western cultures and has had various meanings in religious, esoteric, and even mathematical contexts. Its use in ritual was borrowed from ceremonial magic.

As a potent magical symbol, the pentacle is used to bring added protection to rituals and to the circle in general, as well as consecrating other ritual tools and charging ingredients for spellwork. The symbol itself is often inscribed on ritual tools and may be drawn in the air during rituals to add more power to the work. Witches may also wear a pentacle on a cord or chain during ritual, or even as part of their daily dress (more on this in "Ritual Jewelry," on pages 100–101).

Unfortunately, a related symbol—the inverse pentagram, with a downward-facing point, has been adopted by contemporary Satanists and is therefore considered to be an image of evil. As noted in part one, Wiccans do not believe in the Christian construct of "the Devil" and this purported figure has no place in Wiccan spirituality, but this point is often missed by those who lump the two practices together, and the shared symbolism in this case doesn't help matters. Prior to its use by Satanic groups, the inverse pentagram simply had different symbolic meaning from the star in its upright position, but, much like the ancient swastika, it's all but impossible now for this symbol to escape negative associations. Nonetheless, some Wiccan covens still make use of it.

Your pentacle can be any size, although generally it is small enough to fit comfortably on the altar with the other tools. It may be ornately carved and/or set with semiprecious gemstones, or it may be a clean and simple design. There are beautiful versions in Wiccan supply shops, but you can also make your own pentacle slab by painting the symbol on a round, flat rock or piece of wood. In a pinch, you can find a basic pentacle symbol online to print out and color, and then glue it to a disk-shaped piece of wood or even sturdy cardboard.

Note: If you do purchase an ornately carved pentacle with other symbols in addition to the pentacle symbol, be sure that you know what each symbol represents. Many symbols may actually be sigils that are created from several individual symbols. Sigils may represent planets, elements, zodiac symbols, or specific magical intentions.

Like the five-pointed star, all symbols contain their own unique energies, which you may or may not want to include in your ritual or magical work. You may find yourself drawn to sigils that resonate with some aspect of your personal path. If so, it's still wise to find out their meaning before incorporating them into your practice.

An influence from ceremonial magic, the athame is a ritual knife that resembles a simple dagger, with a black handle and a double-edged blade. The blade is typically about the length of one's hand, or shorter. Many practitioners keep a dull athame because it's not generally used as a cutting tool, but rather for directing energy in ritual. Others keep the blade well sharpened in order to direct that energy more powerfully.

Like the wand, the athame may be used to draw the circle before ritual and close the circle afterward. However, due to its sharp edges, it is more of an energy manipulator or commander, as opposed to an energy conductor. Therefore, the athame isn't typically used to invoke deities, as this would be considered forceful, rather than collaborative, in terms of working with divine energy.

The athame is also used to draw magical symbols, such as the pentagram, in the air to lend power to ritual and spellwork, and is often employed in rituals that banish and/or release negative energies or influences. This tool is associated with the God and the element of Fire (or Air, in some traditions), as it is an agent that causes change.

Depending on the tradition, the athame may do double duty as an actual cutting and engraving tool. It may be used to cut herbs, shape a new wand from the branch of a tree, or carve magical symbols into a candle for ritual use. However, many Witches prefer to use a *boline* for these purposes, keeping the athame for ritual use only. In some traditions, the handle of the athame can be used as a tool for storing energy, which may be used later for ritual and/or magical purposes.

When choosing an athame, be sure to spend some time holding each knife you're considering in your hand. Consider the carvings on the handle (if any) and whether it seems practical for your ritual space. Pick one that you can firmly grasp while casting circles, drawing pentacles, or consecrating other tools, as you don't want to have an accident!

It's fine to take cost into consideration, too. The price of store-bought ritual knives may range from reasonably affordable to extravagantly expensive. If you're on a tight budget, remember that you can turn any "ordinary" object into a ritual tool with the right energy and intent. It may be that you have a perfect knife to consecrate as an athame in your kitchen drawer right now!

If you like, you can enhance your energetic connection with your new athame by carving magical symbols into the handle. One caveat here is that it's considered unwise to use a knife that has been used to cut animal flesh. If this is your only choice, however, know that any negative energies lingering from such use can be ritually cleansed before "converting" the knife into an athame.

Whether you purchase or "repurpose" your athame, the most important thing to consider, of course, is how it feels in your hand. As with any ritual tool, if the energy of the knife doesn't feel positive, then it's safe to say it's not meant for you.

Chalice/Cup

The chalice, known in some traditions as the goblet, or simply, the cup, is another tool borrowed from ceremonial magic, although it also has symbolic significance in Christianity, Sufism, and Arthurian legend. Symbolic of fertility, abundance, and divine

feminine energy, the chalice is sacred to the Goddess and aligned with the Element of Water. It is traditionally silver in color, in honor of the Goddess, but can be made of any quality substance such as earthenware, crystal, or glass.

The chalice may hold water, wine (or juice, for those who don't drink alcohol), or possibly a special tea brewed for the magical purpose of the rite. It is used to offer libations to the deities, and in coven rituals it is shared among all the members during the cakes and ale ceremony. It may remain empty on some occasions, however, as a symbol of readiness to receive blessings from the Universe.

Your chalice can take the form of a grand and ornately decorated vessel or a simple short-stemmed wine glass. Just know that the shiny silver or brass (or silver- or brass-plated) chalices in Wiccan shops will eventually need polishing, so consider whether this is too high-maintenance for you. Also, older metal drinking vessels are likely to contain lead, so be careful about thrift store purchases as well. If you plan to drink wine from your chalice, make sure it's not made of anything that can leach chemicals into the wine.

You might simply dedicate a favorite old family cup or mug to the purpose, charging it with magical energy and keeping it just for ritual. The accumulated positive energy associated with such an heirloom can be more powerful than that of a new chalice, no matter how fancy it might be, if you don't feel attached to it. Whatever you choose, keep your chalice entirely separate from your everyday drinking vessels. Don't put it in the dishwasher—wash it by hand and keep it with your other ritual tools.

Incense

Used for thousands of years in many religious traditions around the world, incense is an ancient ritual tool that harnesses the aromatic and energetic powers of various herbs, spices, oils, resins, and tree barks.

Many Witches feel that incense is an essential component to successful ritual. This is partly due to the consciousness-altering potential of quality incense, which can facilitate a more focused state of mind when performing magical work.

Smoldering incense is often placed before images of the deities on an altar or a shrine. It is often carried around the circle when invoking the East and the Element of Air. It's also used for consecration, purifying items, and as a scrying tool—smoke from the incense may provide visions of the deities invoked in ritual, or other images pertinent to the work being performed.

Furthermore, certain herbs, spices, barks, and roots have specific magical qualities, so homemade incense blends can be used to strengthen magical spells. Incense is associated with the Element of Air, though some may place it with Fire, since it must be ignited to burn.

TYPES OF INCENSE

Incense comes in many forms, from traditional "raw" incense to granulated and powdered varieties. Incense sticks and cones are the most familiar to the average person, but Traditional Wiccan practices favor loose incense. These blends of dried and crumpled herbs, wood shavings, oils, and/or small granules of resin are fun to use and very easy to make, although burning them requires more assembly and attention.

Loose incense doesn't tend to burn for as long as other types, but it has a delightfully Earth-y aesthetic, as you can see literally every ingredient in the blend. It's very important that loose, burning incense is not disturbed, since smoldering pieces can fairly easily ignite or burn holes in fabric and other surfaces. Loose incense also comes in powdered form and tends to burn even faster than the traditional loose variety, but it is less unpredictable when burning.

Some Wiccans find loose incense a bit too much to deal with on a regular basis, and may reserve its use for highly important rituals, if they use it at all. Many prefer sticks and cones, which are made of the same combustible materials, but burn more slowly over a period of time and are less labor intensive. It's fine to use whichever you prefer or have on hand, although if you've never worked with loose incense, it's worth giving it a try.

Resins are another form of incense that has been used around the world in sacred ceremonies for thousands of years. These sticky granules are made with the refined sap of trees and plants and have very strong and clean fragrances. Like loose incense, they require some extra equipment to burn (see below).

Finally, smudge sticks, while not technically considered incense, can be used for similar purposes. They're made up of bundles of partially dried herbs that smolder well. The most common smudge sticks contain sage, and are often used in house cleansing and purification rites. When using a smudge stick to cast the circle, it's best to leave it smoldering in a heat-resistant dish and use a feather to fan the smoke around, so that embers don't drop to the floor and cause burns.

To use traditional loose incense or resins, you'll need a censer or other heat-resistant dish as well as charcoal tablets and sand. The censer can be a traditional swinging censer suspended from chains, like those used in the Catholic church, or a simpler construction, depending on whether the incense is moved around during the ritual. Some Witches may let the incense smolder in the cauldron in lieu of a censer. The most important thing is to make sure the dish is heat and shatter proof, and that it sits on a trivet to keep it from overheating the surface of the altar.

There are definite safety precautions to take when using charcoal—namely, avoid starting a fire, but also be sure to use the correct type of charcoal. Buy charcoal tablets specifically designed to burn incense and herbs. (These can usually be found anywhere you can buy loose incense.) Charcoal briquettes are for outdoor barbecuing and let off some extremely toxic fumes and byproducts when burned, so never use them for incense!

Self-lighting charcoal tablets contain saltpeter, which is thought to be potentially toxic and can make the tablets burn at a higher than ideal temperature for incense. On the plus side, they're generally easier to work with, especially for beginners. More experienced Witches typically prefer tablets made with traditional, additive-free charcoal. These require more time to ignite, but the result is cleaner burning and more fragrant incense.

Sand is another necessity if you are working with loose or powdered incense and resins. It's excellent for absorbing heat, extinguishing flame and embers, and providing a safe bed for smoldering charcoal cakes to sit on. You can gather sand for free from beaches, riverbeds, or even playgrounds. Alternatively, try craft stores, or better yet, visit your local gardening store, where you might be given a good deal on just a couple pounds of sand.

To burn your incense, pour a generous layer of sand into the censer and lay a charcoal tablet on top. Then ignite the charcoal and place a generous pinch of the incense directly onto it. Alternatively, if you find that the charcoal burns the incense too quickly, you can get a mica tablet to act as a barrier from the intense heat. Mica is a type of mineral with a smooth surface that makes a perfect "stove top" for burning oils, loose incense, powders, and resins. Your mica tablet should sit easily on top of the charcoal, where it will essentially simmer the herb mixture instead of scorching it.

OTHER INCENSE AND ACCESSORIES

If loose incense seems like an impractical proposition, you can always take a simpler approach with sticks or cones. Incense sticks can be bought nearly everywhere, but the quality of their ingredients varies from excellent to downright toxic. Choose incense with a comprehensive ingredient list that contains items like essential oils, ground herbs, and resins. Make sure there are no synthetic fragrances (or "fragrance oils") in the blend. The same goes for cones, which are also fairly widely available.

Both sticks and cones require a heat-resistant dish to catch the ash as it falls from the burning incense. Stick incense works best in a "boat" (a holder shaped somewhat like a canoe), or a long tray with a hole in one end for inserting the non-burning end of the stick. There are other, smaller types of holders for stick incense, but they tend to leave more of a mess, and have a higher risk of burning holes in your altar cloth.

Cone incense can be burned in any type of shallow, heat-resistant dish—even a small plate will do, if you don't mind possible scorch marks. You could also use an ashtray or an abalone shell. There are also plenty of nice holders made specifically for cone incense. Be aware that brass or copper holders will heat up, which is risky when you're walking the circle with it or otherwise moving it around. Many Witches enjoy using three-legged cone holders for their resemblance to cauldrons.

Note: Those who have asthma, allergies, or other sensitivities to incense smoke are not likely to embrace this particular component of Wiccan ritual. The good news, however, is that you can use fragrant essential oils in place of incense, whether via an oil burner, a diffuser, or an anointed candle. Plenty of traditional incense scents have essential oil counterparts, including frankincense, myrrh, cinnamon, and lavender. The candle can serve as the Air representation on your altar. (If you are using a diffuser or burner, you can use an alternative Air representation.)

Cauldron

While the word "cauldron" may bring to mind images of Shakespeare's three witches tossing all kinds of animal parts into a boiling stew for evil purposes, the cauldron is really a symbol of the Goddess and the creative forces of transformation.
In some traditions, the cauldron's three legs are associated with the three phases of the Triple Goddess, or the phases of the birth/death/rebirth cycle.

Cauldrons appear in many ancient Celtic myths in connection with magical occurrences and continue to influence Witchcraft today. Associated with the element of Water, the cauldron has many potential uses in both ritual and magic. It may be used to burn loose incense, hold magically charged ingredients for a potion, or allow spell candles to burn out. It can also be filled with fresh water and used for scrying. While some Witches may actually brew a magical potion right in the cauldron, the practical constraints of lighting a safe indoor fire underneath it tend to limit this use—the "brewing" aspect of such magic is often more symbolic than literal.

Cast iron is considered the ideal material for the cauldron, although other metals may be used. You can find many options in Wiccan supply shops, with smaller versions that are typically more affordable. The opening in most cauldrons is smaller in diameter than the widest part of the bowl. Cauldrons can be anywhere from a few inches to a few feet across in diameter, although larger sizes may be considered impractical, depending on your ritual space. The classic double-handled design is ideal, as its curved edges help contain candle flames, and because most cauldrons are still made of cast iron, there's little chance of shattering. Your cauldron should have feet, and if it's small enough to sit on the altar, it should sit on a trivet to keep it from damaging your altar-top.

Unlike other ritual tools, such as the athame and chalice, cauldrons aren't exactly easy to replicate with something around your house—at least, not if you want to use them for anything involving heat. If you can't get your hands on one, don't worry about it. As long as you have a chalice to represent the Goddess on your altar, the cauldron can be considered an optional element of your practice.

Cake Plate

The cake plate can be any ordinary plate, or something special, like a piece of china. It should always be kept separate from any tools or other items that touch anything inedible—like poisonous herbs, oils, incense, or other ingredients you may be using in spell-work. If you are on your own, you can use a small dish, but covens should have a large enough dish to hold an entire group's worth of cakes or other bite-size offerings.

As for the "cakes" themselves, they don't really have to be cakes. Traditionally, Witches would make oatcakes for this purpose, but you can make any sort of cookie or biscuit or use fruit or even crudités. Covens may have their own preferences according their traditions (and any allergies), but solitary practitioners can go for whatever makes them feel comfortable.

Depending on how much room you have, the cakes may be placed on the altar or nearby, within the circle, until it's time for cakes and ale. The ritual beverage may be placed in the chalice from the start of ritual or kept in a separate jug and poured into the chalice at the appropriate time.

OPTIONAL/ADJUNCT
RITUAL ITEMS

WHILE THE ITEMS DESCRIBED ON PAGES 90–98 ARE GENER-ally considered "optional," some might actually be considered essential by particular covens and individual practitioners (especially the broom and the bell). Yet these items may or may not be used in formal ritual. Some have an adjunct role to play, as divination tools and ambient music, for example, while others merely assist in a practical way. But all are items that can be used to enhance the overall ritual experience. As you read about each item, below, pay special attention to the ones that resonate with you.

Broom

Perhaps the most common (and most commonly misunderstood) symbol of Witches and Witchcraft in popular culture, the broom has been part of Wiccan and other pagan lore around the world for centuries. Yet, as associated with all things Witchy as the broom may be, it can be considered an optional tool, depending on your preferences.

Known traditionally as a "besom," the sacred broom is not necessarily used in formal Wiccan ritual itself; instead it is used, metaphorically, to sweep energetic clutter from the ritual space

beforehand: The bristles don't actually have to make contact with the floor. In fact, in some traditions, the broom is never supposed to touch it. Any cleansing occurs on the psychic and energetic level. Like smudge sticks, the besom is a tool for preparing a place for ritual and other spiritual activity, and using it in this way can have a calming, meditative effect on the person doing the "sweeping."

Because it serves as a purifier, the broom is associated with the element of Water and is sacred to the Goddess. It also has protective properties and can be placed near the entrance to a home to guard against negative or unwanted energy. The broom can also be used to help close the circle once you're ready to dismiss the Quarters—and it can be highly effective at dissipating the energies of the work. During ritual, the broom will usually sit to the side of the altar.

Your besom can be any size, from the miniature "decorative" broom that people hang on doors to a more conventional one with a full-length broomstick. If you opt for a hand-made besom, traditional woods include birch, ash, and willow. Alternatively, you can use a long tree branch with several twigs on the end to serve the purpose.

Of course, while many Witches keep hand-made brooms for ritual purposes, a common household broom can also be dedicated to the work of Witchcraft. However, it should never be used for everyday housecleaning, as this would contaminate the sacred energy it holds for ritual and magical purposes. So treat yourself to a new broom, as this is one tool that isn't suited to having a "past life" in the mundane world.

Sword and/or Staff

In some traditions, a ritual sword is used in place of, or sometimes in addition to, the athame. Swords have been mentioned in magical texts dating back to the Middle Ages, and feature in many tales from Celtic and Germanic mythology.

Swords are not nearly as easily obtainable as knives, which may account for their relative rarity in Wiccan practice. However, they're also rather impractical for indoor use, due to their size. The sword is typically reserved for highly formalized ritual occasions and is used, ideally, in large outdoor spaces where the participants can remain at a safe remove from the Witch that is wielding it. In coven rituals, the High Priest and/or Priestess holds the sword. The hilt may be any color, but as it is technically a type of athame, many Wiccans prefer black. The hilt or the blade may be engraved with magical symbols.

The sword may be used for drawing the circle and is particularly effective for protection and banishing negative energy. Like the athame, the sword is a masculine tool associated with the God. Depending on the tradition its Elemental correspondence may be Air or Fire.

A staff is also sometimes used in formal ritual, typically held by the High Priest or Priestess of a coven, although plenty of solitary Witches work with a staff. The staff has a longer history of ritual use than most of the other Wiccan tools, going all the way back to ancient Egypt. It is traditionally carved from a long and sturdy tree branch and is long enough to serve as a walking stick. It may be carved with magical symbols and/or decorated with small bells, ribbons, crystals, leaves, or shells.

Like the wand, which is really just a shorter version of the staff, it is a channeler of energy and can be used to draw the circle and/or invoke the Element of Air or Fire, depending on the tradition. It is a symbol of power, authority, and skill in working with the energies of Nature. The staff is associated with either Fire or Air and is sacred to the God in most traditions.

Bell

The bell, also known as a "witch's bell" (or, in some traditions, a "devil driver"), can serve a variety of purposes, whether or not it is incorporated into formal ritual. Witch's bells resemble those used by the town criers of old. They are nearly always made of heavy-gauge metal and have a solid wood handle. They can be made of brass or steel and may be decorated with silver or gold plating and/or etchings and engravings.

Many Wiccans associate the bell's musicality with the Element of Air, while others attribute it to Water, in honor of the waves of sound that emanate from the bell as it is rung. Either way, the bell is widely associated with the Goddess.

Those who use the bell in rituals may ring it three times after casting the circle and before beginning work at the altar. Others will ring the bell three times before casting their circle to declare the start of the ritual. The bell may be used to call to the God and Goddess, to emphasize the focal points of ritual prayers, and even to "seal" any spellwork that is performed. Some Witches ring the bell over their ritual tools and spell ingredients to clear them of old or unwanted energy. It can also be used to clear any living or working space, as the vibrations radiating from the sound will scatter any stale energetic blocks.

You can find hand bells at music stores, craft stores, and even the home decorating aisle in some big box stores, as well as many Wiccan supply shops. Ideally, a bell is the one tool that you should buy in person, as you want to be sure that you'll like the way it sounds. If you purchase a bell online, be sure to check how much it weighs in the item description. Lighter bells won't resonate with sound as nicely as heavier ones.

Divination Tools

Many Witches also incorporate divination tools in their ritual practice. These may include runes, Tarot cards, a quartz crystal sphere (or "crystal ball") for scrying, or other oracles borrowed from older traditions, such as the I-Ching. Divination may take place during a formal ritual, but post-ritual is also considered a good time for this activity, as the Witch is still in a conducive state of mind to communicate with the Spirit world.

Divination is completely optional, and if you don't already practice it, there's no requirement to learn how! However, if you do use divination—or even if you're just learning a divination method— you might design your rituals to include time for this practice.

Book of Shadows

If you're just starting out, you probably don't have much material for a Book of Shadows of your own yet. Like many beginners, you're likely using ritual formats, words, and/or other ideas from one or more books on Wicca. Nonetheless, it's a good idea to plan out your rituals in a blank book as you prepare to perform them, along with any spells you're trying from other sources. This work will serve as the beginning of your first Book of Shadows, and help you remember the words and actions associated with each step of your rituals.

You can use a plain old notebook or a blank journal, or you can buy a specially designed Book of Shadows from a Wiccan shop to write in. Feel free to enhance the aura of your Book by using specially designated pens or pencils to write in it. You may keep the Book of Shadows on the altar during ritual, or near enough to read from it, as you work.

Ambient Music

Music is an extremely powerful vehicle for spirituality. Shamanic traditions around the world employ drums, "rain sticks," and other hand-made acoustic instruments to make contact with the non-physical realms. These same instruments can enhance the atmosphere of ritual, whether for chanting, dancing, raising energy, or simply creating a mood of celebration for a Sabbat gathering.

Meditation and other ambient music recordings are also good enhancements, especially if you're having trouble grounding and centering before casting your circle. So don't feel that your Craft must be practiced in silence. Just be sure that whatever you choose to play or listen to is peaceful and positive.

Altar Cloth

Your altar might be a very special, ornately designed antique, or you might choose something a bit more humble—like your living room coffee table. Whatever the case, because of the materials you're working with—oils, herbs, incense, and candles—you will undoubtedly encounter some kind of mess at one point or another, so keep that in mind as you make your selection.

An altar cloth protects the surface of your altar from burns, wax, and oil staining. (For those of you whose altars are doing double-duty as ordinary furniture, it can also help create a sense of sacred space.) It can be as plain or as pretty as you like, but you may want to stick to a fabric that's washable, so you won't be heartbroken, if it gets ruined by accident. If you want to go all-out, you can have multiple, different-colored altar cloths to correspond with the seasonal energies of the nearest Sabbat. However, using an altar cloth is completely up to you.

Anointing Oils

The use of anointing (or "botanical") oils—either single oils or blends—are essential in rituals and spellwork for a variety of purposes, including anointing the Goddess and God candles and other ritual tools, consecrating new tools, marking your third eye before divination, and more.

Many of the botanical oils used in Wiccan ritual and spellwork have been used for spiritual purposes since the days of the Old Testament, where you'll find references to myrrh, cinnamon, cassia, and olive oils used for anointing sacred items. Like herbs, crystals, and colors, plant-based oils have specific energetic properties linking them to different deities, Sabbats, types of ritual, and all kinds of spellwork. You can find specially blended oils for all kinds of purposes at any Wiccan shop.

Generally, the oil used for anointing deity candles and other altar tools is reserved specifically for that purpose—oils used in other ritual work and/or spellwork are kept separately. Because they are volatile and can be flammable in some cases, keep oils away from heat sources, and always store them in dark glass bottles. When shopping for essential oils, always read the labels. Avoid anything that includes synthetic or "fragrance" oils, as these can actually be toxic, and they don't contribute naturally derived magical energy to the work.

Quality essential oils can be hard on the budget, however, so if need be, you can make your own anointing oil from olive oil infused with fresh or dried herbs instead. However, this kind of oil will go rancid much sooner than properly made essential oils, so you'll want to make small batches at a time.

Fire Accessories

Note: It's not necessary to keep these items on your altar, but it is helpful to have them nearby.

Candlesnuffer: Extinguishing candles safely, and in a manner respectful to the Element of Fire, is an important consideration in Wiccan practice. The modern tradition of birthday candles notwithstanding, there are taboos in many magical traditions against blowing out a flame with your breath. Some people use their fingers to snuff out candles, and others wave their hands over the flame until it goes out. These methods can be hazardous due to the obvious risk of burns—as well as knocking things over or lighting a sleeve on fire. A candlesnuffer is a clean and elegant way to solve the issue and will make your candles last longer as well.

Long Matches or a Grill Lighter: Lighting candles, incense, and charcoal can be difficult if you can't reach a candle easily or need a sustained flame. It's best to invest in long-handled matches or a BBQ/grill lighter—they'll make it possible to hold a flame for longer periods of time against cone incense or charcoal, which can take a while to ignite. You can also use them to get into deep jar candles that still have plenty of wick to burn but can't be lit with standard lighters or matches.

Cloth for anointing oil: When anointing candles or other objects, you'll undoubtedly end up with oil on your fingers. Oil is flammable, so it's advisable to wipe off any excess oil with a clean cloth before handling matches or a lighter. If you're using oils that may irritate your skin, you can also use the cloth for the actual anointing, so the oil doesn't touch your fingers.

RITUAL WEAR

MANY WITCHES LIKE TO INCLUDE ENERGETICALLY CHARGED jewelry and other elements of "costume" into their practice—a custom found in many religious traditions throughout the world. Some may simply wear a pentacle on a chain, while others may don special robes and/or a headpiece encrusted with gemstones to enhance their personal energy during ritual. In some traditions, Witches work naked, a practice that is generally referred to as "sky-clad."

It's important to note that unless you are part of a coven with specific requirements, you don't have to wear anything special if you don't want to. Nonetheless, many find that it can boost their confidence in their own personal power to don something specifically designated for spiritual occasions. When used appropriately, ritual wear can enhance the energy of your ritual space, add power to your work, and protect you from unwanted energies. Here are a few of the things that Wiccans might wear when in the circle.

Ritual Robes

Many Witches enjoy honoring the long-standing tradition of working in a robe for ritual occasions. Ritual robes come in many colors, shapes, and materials, and can be custom-made or purchased in off-the-rack sizes. (These robes should not be confused with cloaks that function as a covering, rather than a main garment.)

Avoid flammable fabrics when you choose a robe and be wary of flowing sleeves and floor-length designs. You wouldn't want to light yourself on fire while spiral dancing or walking the circle, so give some thought to your particular ritual space, in addition to fit and comfort, when choosing your robes.

Cloaks

Cloaks are well-suited to outdoor rituals for Sabbats and for doing magic outside on a cold night. They come in several styles and may or may not have sleeves or hoods.

Like ritual robes, cloaks can be custom-made or purchased off-the-rack. If you're particularly eager to have a powerful, one-of-a-kind cloak, you might find a Pagan seamstress or tailor who will take your measurements and work magic into its creation.

Pentacle

As noted earlier, many Wiccans wear a pentacle around their neck during rituals. In fact, many Wiccans wear the pentacle quite regularly, although it may or may not be worn openly, depending on whether or not one is "in the broom closet" about their faith. In some coven traditions, however, new members may not be permitted to wear a pentacle until they have been initiated. Where degree systems are present, the pentacle worn may differ according to which degree the member has attained. For example, new initiates might only wear a plain white disk with the pentacle symbol on it, while second- or third-degree initiates might wear more elegant and decorative designs.

If you're solitary, you may also wish to begin with a small, plain pentacle as you begin your practice, and move to a more ornate version once you feel comfortable with your progress. This is a nice way to honor your personal spiritual journey.

Like any other magical item, pentacles are available from Wiccan retailers in a wide range of styles and prices. You can find beautiful versions made with gold, silver, crystals, and ornate carvings, along with simpler, yet more affordable designs and materials. Just make sure your pentacle doesn't contain any nickel or other metals that can irritate your skin. If you're secret about your faith, but wish to wear a pentacle anyway, consider its size as well as the quality of the chain or cord for easy concealment.

Other Jewelry

Beyond the pentacle, ritual jewelry includes any piece of jewelry that's consecrated for ritual purposes. This can be a ring, bracelet, pendant, necklace, earring, arm cuff . . . even a tiara or crown. Typically, these pieces are made from precious or semiprecious metals, although some Witches enjoy working with bone, wood, and fossilized materials. Ritual jewelry often features crystals, or other gem and mineral stones, and may have engraved sigils or other magical symbols.

Crystal and other mineral-stone jewelry is great for amplifying your rituals and spellwork. Many practitioners have specially designated crystal jewelry for ritual work. Others choose stones that coincide with the work they are about to do within the circle on a given night. Many crystal shops sell cords with small wire enclosures attached, into which you can simply place the stone of your choice. Choose crystals and stones that resonate with you and, ideally, correspond to the aims of your ritual and/or spellwork.

You can find all sorts of crystal jewelry in brick-and-mortar stores and online—they don't even need to be Pagan or "New Age" establishments. Make sure you're dealing with a reputable business though, as certain stones are sometimes found to be cheap imitations. For example, "fake citrine" is produced when amethyst is heated to a certain temperature. As for metal jewelry, keep your eye out for knock-offs and items made with nickel or other irritating materials.

If you are drawn to a certain symbol featured on a piece of jewelry, but aren't sure what it means, do some research before wearing it in ritual. You don't want to wear a sigil with negative intent coded into it or muddle the focus of a spell with mismatched energies.

All that being said, you don't have to purchase new pieces of jewelry for your Wiccan practice. Ritual jewelry can be any piece of jewelry that has personal significance to you, regardless of what it's made of. You don't have to reserve it just for ritual, either, although it's a good idea to cleanse anything you wear regularly prior to ritual use.

Finally, you don't need to wear everything in your jewelry box for a single ritual (though you certainly can if you like!). A single bracelet, ring, or pendant will do just fine. And, of course, you don't need any jewelry at all to create a powerful ritual experience—you need only your own focused energy and intention.

BUILDING YOUR COLLECTION OF RITUAL TOOLS

WHILE IT'S GENERALLY CONSIDERED HELPFUL TO USE AT least a few, if not several, of the tools described above, it is ultimately about the Witch (or coven) and their connection to the specific tools chosen. While some covens and solitaries may create elaborate rituals using every tool imaginable, others may design very simple affairs involving simply a candle and a small representation of each Element.

In other words, it's more about using what feels inspiring and "in tune," rather than gathering items from a checklist. If it feels out of place or unpleasantly strange to a particular Witch to purchase and use a cauldron or wear special robes, then these items may simply not be necessary or suitable for that person.

Keep in mind that you don't have to acquire all of your tools in order to perform your first ritual, so don't feel pressured to rush out and purchase everything at once. Take your time and get to know your new tools gradually as you're learning and getting familiar with your ritual protocol. Your tools will serve you better in the long run if you take this approach. For now, strive for at least one tool to represent each of the Elements. This will promote balanced energy in your rituals.

Wicca is very malleable, and you can adapt things to suit you in a manner that resonates with you. For example, if you have a wand, you don't necessarily need the athame, since either one can serve the functions of the other. If you want to consecrate a wine glass to work with as a chalice, at the moment, and then buy a special silver goblet for the work sometime down the road, that's perfectly fine, too.

Now is a good time to mention that any material object you wish to acquire for your spiritual purposes can be called to you through focused intention. Simply ask the powers that be—you can name the Goddess and/or the God, or whatever deity or other focal point you connect with—to aid you in finding what you need. Then, be sure to pay attention! Visit thrift stores, yard sales, flea markets. and any other place where you know it's possible to discover what you're looking for.

MOVING INTO MAGIC

NOW THAT WE'VE ESTABLISHED THE BASIC FRAMEWORK AND concepts underlying Wiccan ritual practice, it's time to explore the enchanting world of Wiccan magic. In part three, we'll examine what magic actually is, how it works, and how it is used in Wicca.

You'll also find an overview of the most common tools and ingredients used in Wiccan spellwork, as well as information on specific uses for natural ingredients like crystals, herbs, and essential oils. With this knowledge, you'll be ready to try your hand at a simple spell provided in the final section of this book.

A CLEARING
AND CONSECRATION
RITUAL

CLEARING YOUR RITUAL TOOLS OF UNWANTED energy and then consecrating them for ritual use is an essential process and should always be undertaken after acquiring a new tool. While generally done in the same sitting, there are actually two different steps. *Clearing* removes residual energy, as discussed above. *Consecrating* actually programs the innate energy of the object for the purposes you intend. In Wicca, this means joining the energy of the object with the divine forces of Nature, usually as represented by the Goddess and the God.

Below you'll find a very simple and effective ritual for clearing and consecrating. It uses repetitive phrases and sentence structure in order to make it easier to remember. You can certainly adapt it to suit your own personal style. You can consecrate several tools in one sitting, if you like—just take each of them through the steps one at a time.

On your altar, you will need a wand or athame, incense or smudging herbs, a candle to represent Fire, a bowl of water, and a bowl of soil, sand, or salt. It's also good to use your Goddess and God representations, if you have them.

- Of course, when you're just starting out, you clearly run into a bit of a chicken-and-egg dilemma. How can you use your dish of water to clear and consecrate your athame when you haven't yet cleared and consecrated your dish of water? Don't worry, if this is the case—everyone has to start somewhere.

- Choose the tool you feel is most important to work with first and go from there, improvising until you've gotten to all of them. For example, if you haven't cleared and consecrated your wand, you can use your hands to conduct energy instead. Trust that your own personal energy will do the trick, and that the Goddess and God are working with you, welcoming you onto your Wiccan path.

- Begin by casting your circle using your chosen approach (you can consult "Casting the Sacred Circle" in part two, pages 61–63, and the Autumn Equinox ritual in part four, pages 147–51 for ideas). When you are ready to begin, take up your first ritual item, hold it up over your altar, and say:

"I hereby cleanse this (ITEM) in the name of the God and Goddess. May all negative and unwanted energies depart from it here and now!"

- Place the item in the center of your altar, and draw a pentacle over it with your wand, athame, or your hand, saying:

"In the name of the Element of Spirit, I dedicate you to the divine. May you be used to harm none and respect the law of three."

- Next, take up your burning incense or smudge stick, and pass the item through its smoke.

> *"In the name of the Element of Air,*
> *I dedicate you to the divine.*
> *May you be used with and for insight,*
> *bringing joy and clear knowledge."*

- After this, you will move to your Fire candle on your altar. Quickly pass the item over the flame (or through it, if it's highly flame-resistant).

> *"In the name of the Element of Fire,*
> *I dedicate you to the divine.*
> *May you provide protection,*
> *evoking positive energy and courage."*

- Now pick up your dish of water. Sprinkle the item with a small amount (or sprinkle water in a circle around it if this is an item that must be kept dry).

> *"In the name of the Element of Water,*
> *I dedicate you to the divine.*
> *May you fill my actions with compassion,*
> *giving me the gifts of sight,*
> *healing, and dreams."*

- Finally, take a few pinches of soil, sand, or salt, and sprinkle them over the item.

> *"In the name of the Element of Earth,*
> *I dedicate you to the divine.*
> *May you guide me to respect nature,*
> *supplying wisdom and prosperity*
> *to all who are in need."*

* Once more, take up your wand, athame, or use your fingers to draw another pentacle over the item, and say:

"As above, so below. I hereby consecrate you in the name of the Goddess and God."

* (If you work with individual aspects of the Goddess and God, you can use your deities' names here)

"Blessed be!"

PART THREE

WICCAN MAGIC

THE STUDY AND PRACTICE OF AN ANCIENT ART

THE WORD *MAGIC* HAS DIFFERENT MEANINGS TO DIFFERENT people. In mainstream culture, it is often relegated to the realm of fantasy or used in reference to events and circumstances that seem to have no logical cause. In Wicca and many other Pagan spiritual paths, *magic* (or *magick*) is a word used for the phenomena that occur when people consciously participate in the co-creative forces of the Universe by using the subtle energies of Nature to cause desired change in their reality.

Magic is an enormous topic that could probably fill an entire library and is certainly worth deep study. In this brief introduction to magic, however, we'll narrow down the scope to focus on the basic rationale for why magic works, the kinds of magic typically practiced by Wiccans, and what it means to get results from your magical intentions. You'll also find some practical information on the use of magical ingredients. Since this guide is meant to be an introduction to these topics, rather than a spell book, the objective here is to understand the basic concepts outlined below. However, a simple spell is included in the Autumn Equinox ritual provided in part four (pages 147–51), so you'll definitely have a chance to put your new knowledge to work!

PRACTICAL MAGIC

THERE IS A FAIRLY BIG DISTINCTION BETWEEN *RITUAL* MAGIC and *practical* magic. The two can certainly overlap, but the majority of the magic practiced by Wiccans falls into the latter category. Much of Wiccan magic is inspired by a blend of older folk traditions and may be less reminiscent of ceremonial magic than typical Wiccan ritual. It is sometimes referred to as "low magic" to distinguish it from the "high magic" of the ceremonial magicians.

Practical magic may be worked during the course of the ritual, but many Wiccans prefer to keep these activities separate, especially at Sabbat celebrations. Others take these opportunities to work for spiritual as well as material progress, as they reflect on their lives at each point in the Wheel. There are some who argue for a distinction between what they consider to be spirituality-based worship ("Wicca") and more "secular" magical practice ("Witchcraft"), but more often the two are intertwined enough that the distinction isn't particularly useful. However, there are also Wiccans who don't do practical magic at all and may or may not consider what takes place in ritual as "magic."

The types, forms, and intentions of magical work are as varied as every other aspect of Wicca and Witchcraft. Individual workings may involve any combination of actions, tools, words, visualizations, and/or spell ingredients. Witches may make charm bags with magical herbs and crystals, take ritual baths with oils consecrated for a specific purpose, or simply light a symbol-inscribed candle for their intention. Like "raising energy" in a circle, these forms and techniques work with the nonphysical realm to affect change on the physical plane. Traditionally, all magic is worked within the sacred circle, whether as part of ritual or in a separate context. However, many eclectics today don't find the circle necessary, especially for a quick spell or the brewing of a magical tea.

The purpose of the magic can also be anything under the sun that is positive and does no harm. What the Craft is definitely *not* used for is anything that could cause harm to another person or other living being, even unintentionally. Our wishes can often be manipulative when it comes to how they affect other people, even when we don't realize it. Therefore, ritual and spellwork often include safeguards against accidental misuse of magical energy, such as the phrases "for the good of all" and "with harm to none."

Keeping this idea in the forefront of one's mind is important, particularly in light of another basic tenet of Wicca: the Threefold Law. Also known as "The Rule of Three" and The Law of Return," this principle states that whatever Witches send out into the Universe as intent, whether positive or negative, will come back to them three times as great. While some Witches don't subscribe to this particular belief, it is often invoked as a reminder that magical power should be used only for good, and never in the spirit of harm or manipulation.

Wiccans and other Witches will incorporate magical work, as they are able and inclined to do so, into any part of their daily lives. In fact, many Witches consider themselves to be constantly "practicing" their Craft in their daily lives through the use of meditation, magically charged meals and beverages, color choices in clothing and jewelry, nightly candle rituals, and other seemingly "small" enactments of magic. The more one is in tune with the rhythms and energies of the natural world, the more "magical" one's life will seem and feel, and this relationship with the cycles of life is deepened throughout one's life through study and practice.

MAGIC AND SCIENCE

MANY CONTEMPORARY WRITERS ON WITCHCRAFT HAVE pointed out the relevance of new discoveries in the physical sciences that seem to identify what Witches have always known to exist: a symbiotic relationship between mind and matter. This relationship can be viewed from many angles and is probably not entirely understood by anyone, but its existence is clear to practitioners of magic as well as other mind/thought-based disciplines that bring about positive change in one's life.

The traditional worldview of most of Western society for the past few millennia has held that reality is both chaotic and inflexible, created by forces outside of human control. It has also held that the mind is not a physical entity and is separate from what we think of as "matter." (The phrase "mind over matter" illustrates the fundamental division perceived to exist between the two.) What Witches understand, and what science has begun to uncover, is that reality is flexible, and is co-created by and with everything within it, including the mind. Mind is not separate from matter—it is matter in its most basic form.

The power of thought has been illuminated in many books and videos about the Law of Attraction, a "New Age" topic that has recently found popularity among mainstream audiences, celebrities, and even business professionals. The Law states that thoughts attract experiences that reinforce them, so that dwelling on negative circumstances can keep them in place, while focusing on positive experiences creates improved circumstances. Changing one's thoughts is harder than it might seem, which is possibly why so much information and advice regarding the Law of Attraction is currently available.

The Hermetic Principles: A Foundation for Understanding Magic

Witchcraft can be said to employ the Law of Attraction in a sense, though magic can be much more complex than simply focusing one's thoughts on a desired outcome. It might be more accurate to say that Witches employ rituals, tools, words, and gifts from the natural world to enhance or expand their magical reach, while also utilizing a body of esoteric knowledge known as the Hermetic Principles.

The Hermetic Principles date back to late antiquity and have informed Western religious, philosophical, esoteric, and scientific thought. They have interesting parallels in modern physics, including quantum mechanics and string theory, and describe the way reality operates at the most basic level of existence, where all material things are composed of energy and radiate energy. Many Witches have been watching excitedly as the scientific understanding of the makeup of the Universe unfolds to confirm what ancient observers knew.

There are seven Hermetic Principles (also known as "Hermetic Laws") that are often referred to in discussions of magic. One of the most emphasized is the *Principle of Correspondence,* which states that what is true on the macrocosm is also true on the microcosm.

This means that every particle in all existence is fundamentally connected to all others—and that linear time on the physical plane represents only one dimension in the ultimately spaceless and timeless overall Universe. Another way of stating the principle is "as above, so below; as below, so above." The higher planes of existence influence the lower planes of existence, and vice versa. As microcosms of the Universe, we are able to glean information from the distant past, view images of the future through divination, and change our reality.

A recent and widely reported study found that the laws governing the growth of the Universe share significant similarities to the growth of both the human brain and the Internet. This is an interesting illustration of the Law of Correspondence, and also provides a window into the *Principle of Mentalism,* another important principle of Witchcraft.

Not only is every particle in existence interconnected, but matter and energy also contain *information* (which is described as "light" in some New Age philosophies) at their most basic level. The Universe, ultimately, is mental at its highest level: it is the underlying creative force of all things. We know that all the inventions, developments, and adaptations in our human history began as ideas. Witches also know that thoughts can influence the Universal mind, and this is part of why focused intention in ritual is important.

The *Principle of Vibration* holds that everything is in constant motion, and that nothing is at rest. This applies even to seemingly sturdy physical objects such as chairs and tables—they have vibrations that we simply can't perceive with the human mind. Matter is composed of energy that is essentially a force moving at a certain vibration. The parallel with animism is worth noting here, as animists believe that everything is alive. If a characteristic of being "alive" is to be in motion, then the animists have been correct all along.

The nature of colors as light moving at different rates of vibration is particularly useful in Witchcraft, as each color's frequency has particular characteristics suitable for specific purposes. We often associate love with the colors red and pink, for example, and it turns out that these colors resonate with energies in the body that promote loving feelings. Therefore, these colors, when used in spellwork to bring love into one's life, both communicate that information to the Universe and connect it to the Witch's energy field.

Of course, like all things, colors can have their down sides. The intense vibration of red can also overstimulate and trigger unpleasant feelings. Color therapy, using the Chakra system and meditation techniques, seeks to balance out-of-whack vibrations in the body, and colors can be used magically in much the same way.

The Law of Attraction itself is mentioned in the Kybalion in the context of the *Principle of Cause and Effect*. Given the nature of reality as described by Hermeticism, it follows that the thoughts, visions, and intentions we send out into the Universe are vibrations that will attract circumstances that bring about the reality we're focused upon. Magic is a very focused way to communicate these intentions, and its effectiveness is amplified by our *knowing* that it works.

WHAT DOES MANIFESTATION LOOK LIKE?

WHEN WITCHES SPEAK OF "MANIFESTATION" OR "SUCCESS" in relation to prayer, intention, or spellwork, what do they really mean? You don't tend to hear fairytale-like stories about enormous, overnight gains in one's quality of life the day after working a spell, although anything can happen if all the right circumstances are in place.

What advanced practitioners of the Craft understand is that *practice* is necessary—in the form of time, study, and experiment. One also has to cultivate a mindset that is open to manifestation, to success, and to magical and positive occurrences. This can be a difficult habit to acquire and hold onto, and everyone has blind spots now and again, but with active practice, the wonders of the Universe begin to unfold more steadily.

Once upon a time, a young, aspiring Witch met an older, much more experienced Witch at a folk festival, where they were both camping in the woods. As the festival wound down and everyone was packing up to leave, the two Witches decided to exchange their contact information. Neither had a writing implement, nor could they find any in their tents or packs. Then suddenly, the younger Witch spotted a pencil "randomly" lying on the forest floor between two trees. "Wow," said the older Witch. "Talk about manifesting!"

The younger Witch was confused. How was this an example of "manifesting"? The pencil hadn't fallen from the sky or even been suddenly delivered by a passerby out of the blue. Sure, it was a welcome coincidence, but clearly some other person had simply lost a pencil in that spot in the woods, and over a festival weekend, those woods saw their fair share of human artifacts. Furthermore, no spell or incantation had been performed. So how did this pencil count as a manifestation?

The younger Witch was too accustomed to analyzing the possible causes of events to appreciate the synchronicity and Divine timing of this pencil's emergence into her reality. Rather than focusing on the inherent magic of this small event, she instinctively moved to dismiss it in favor of the habitual "rational" thinking instilled in her through cultural conditioning. This is a challenge faced by many who are new to the Craft, but with persistent willingness to be open to the subtleties of reality underneath our "rational" experience, it becomes easier to recognize all kinds of manifestations, from the "little things" to much larger transformations in our lives.

There are a few key elements in this particular incident that meet the conceptual requirements of manifestation. First, the pencil appeared in the right place at the right time. Second, it fulfilled a specific need that, if met, would be beneficial to both people involved, and would harm no one. Third, it happened in a way that was unexpected, rather than as a result of looking in all the obvious, logical places for something to write with. Manifestation often comes in ways we never could have imagined or planned for. And as an extra-nice touch, it happened in a natural setting: a forest of old, magnificent trees.

Just as importantly, the pencil was *acknowledged* as a manifestation by the older Witch, who knew from practice how to recognize and appreciate it as such. She also knew that manifestation could happen with or without designated spellwork. Sometimes the Universe simply helps out in moments of need or crisis—these occasions are sometimes called "miracles." Since the older Witch was well grounded in magical principles, she was often able to intend for things immediately and did so habitually, always growing in her ability to connect her personal power with the Divine.

Beyond spellwork, ritual, and intention-setting, the practice of paying attention and acknowledging with gratitude is just as important to successful manifestation. As you start seeing synchronicities in your life, however small, take note and remember them. You may want to record incidents that seem significant in a journal or Book of Shadows. You will find that the more you pay attention to them, the more you will attract positive manifestation in your life.

TOOLS AND INGREDIENTS IN WICCAN MAGIC

MAGIC CAN TAKE MANY DIFFERENT FORMS IN WICCA, BUT the main branches of this ancient art revolve around candles, crystals, herbs, "spell crafts"—the making of charms and other magical items—and other methods of working with tangible things. On pages 121–26 is a list of staple tools and ingredients to get you started in these and other forms of magic. Note that some ritual tools might also be used in certain forms of practical magic, and some of the items here can be used as part of Wiccan ritual, such as when marking the sacred circle with crystals or herbs.

If yet another list of things to acquire in order to practice Wicca feels overwhelming at this point, just remember that these are optional, and that you should follow your intuition regarding where—or even whether—to start. Remember, not all Wiccans actually practice magic. Some are simply drawn to honor Nature in the special way that the religion of Wicca offers, and choose to leave it at that.

If you do want to learn magic as part of your personal practice, don't be afraid to start small. Perhaps you want to work with candle spells for a while before moving on to learning about crystals. Or perhaps you don't feel drawn to crystals at all; in which case, there's no need to acquire any! Just take a look, listen to your gut, and start with what makes sense to you. You can always return to this list to try new things as you grow in your practice.

Crystals, Herbs, and Oils

Perhaps some of the most powerful magical tools are those that come straight from the Earth without much, if any, alteration by human hands. Herbs, crystals, and mineral stones have long been known to have healing properties and are used today in many medicinal systems around the globe. They are also used in Witchcraft, as decorations, offerings, magical enhancements, and even as the focus of some rituals and spells.

Crystals and Mineral Stones: Crystals and minerals are powerful items for magic for those who resonate with these Earth energies. Much more than mere "rocks," crystals and other stones have their own energies and are considered to be "alive," rather than simply dormant matter.

Sensitive people can often feel their energies when holding these stones in their hands or on some other part of their bodies. Some stones are used for specific purposes in ritual, while others may be more permanent presences on the altar or in other places in a Witch's home. They may range in size from a square half-inch to much larger and may be polished and/or carved into specific shapes or left in their raw form. Crystals can be found in many New Age stores as well as online, although they can sometimes still be found in their raw form in certain natural areas.

Crystals may be used to help guard against illness or negative energy or may aid in divination or other psychic work. They may also be used to lay out the magic circle at the start of ritual. These stones have astrological associations as well as associations with specific deities and Elements.

Every crystal and mineral stone has specific magical purposes for which it is ideal, so before you purchase stones, it can be useful to do some research into what will help you the most with your goal. There are many books and online resources detailing crystals and their magical properties. However, if you're browsing crystals in a store and feel called to a particular stone, that's a good sign that it's meant for you. As mentioned earlier, however, beware of counterfeits—rarer stones like amber and jet are sometimes just dyed glass.

Herbs: Herbs are also associated with specific deities and astrological bodies, and are used in a variety of forms, including magical kitchen edibles, brews and potions, incense blends, and on their own as simple spell ingredients. Some of the most common kitchen herbs, such as basil, rosemary, and thyme also have magical associations that double their potential for effective magic, as they can be used to make "enchanted" foods. However, other herbs used in magic are not appropriate to consume, and care should always be taken to know the difference.

It is considered ideal for Witches to harvest their own herbs with a boline, whether from nearby woods, their own gardens, or potted plants in the windowsill. However, fresh herbs can be found in grocery stores, and many natural food stores also sell a variety of dried herbs.

Oils: The oils derived from plants, seeds, and nuts are used to enhance ritual atmosphere and also as ingredients in spellwork. Oils have metaphysical properties and may be rubbed into spell candles for a specific magical purpose or used in a skin-safe blend to anoint the body before ritual.

Witches often make their own blends of essential oils to strengthen ritual and spellwork. Also used in aromatherapy for healing a number of physical and emotional ailments, essential oils are widely available at natural food stores.

Candles

You can never have too many candles when practicing Wicca, particularly when it comes to spellwork. Candles are a simple and direct way to work with color magic. Colors have their own metaphysical properties, as well as astrological and Elemental associations that are detailed in the Table of Correspondence: Colors, on pages 130–31.

Candles used for specific spell purposes are usually left to burn out on their own and, consequently, tend to be smaller. Beeswax, tapers, votives, and tea light candles can all be used, although some stores sell individual candles that are sized and colored specifically for spellwork. These candles are usually no more than four inches tall and less than one half-inch in diameter.

You can also buy special seven-day candles that have notches for sections that measure one day's worth of burning (you can also carve the notches yourself, using your athame). Although specially charged candles are more expensive, they can carry greater power. It may be worth looking into these, particularly for beginners who are just trying out candle magic for the first time.

Other Items Used in Spellwork

Parchment: When we speak of parchment in Wicca, we aren't referring to the kind you would use to line a cake pan. Parchment is paper that can be written on and burned or buried. You can find parchment that's specially made and pressed with flowers in it, which is good for those who like to use flower correspondences in their spells.

Magic Cord and Ribbon: Magic cord and ribbon can be used for different purposes based on their colors. Typically, you would use cordage and ribbons for "binding" spells, knot magic, Beltane celebrations, tying up sprigs of herbs for aspersing or smudge bundles, and hanging fresh herbs to dry.

Empty Bottles and Jars: Witches love jars and bottles for their versatility and usefulness in spells and rituals. Often, you can simply repurpose emptied food jars that would otherwise land in the recycling bin, but for some purposes, you may need to purchase a particular size, shape, or color. It's best to have small vials for potions; small bottles with dark glass for oil blends and homemade perfumes; and large jars for large spells, storing dried herbs and incense, and making items like holy water, moon water, and solar water. As with the mortar and pestle, you will want to have separate jars for separate purposes. Inedible herbs and poisonous oils should never come in contact with any vessel you wish to eat or drink from. To ensure that no cross-contamination occurs, get labels for all jars and bottles used in magic.

Fabrics and Sewing Materials: If you'd like to work with poppets (handmade dolls used in Witchcraft), talismans, herb sachets, or dream pillows, you will need to invest in a few pieces of fabric and some basic sewing materials. You don't have to have a sewing machine or be an adept tailor. Basic items like needles, thread, embroidery floss, scissors, and pins will do.

Divination Tools: Those who read Tarot cards may incorporate a specific card into a spell, based on its meaning and relevance to the purpose at hand. Runes can be used in much the same way. Illustrated Tarot cards may also be used for visualization purposes when preparing for spellwork or as part of the spell itself.

Boline: A boline is a special knife that's used for spells and other practical purposes. It is separate and very different from an athame, which is meant just for rituals. The boline is a single-bladed knife that usually has a white handle. Some bolines are very ornate (much like athames), but this almost always depends on the type of Wicca you practice and whether you are on your own or in a coven. The boline can be used for cutting, carving, and slicing ingredients in preparation for spells and rituals.

Mortar & Pestle: A two-part tool, the mortar and pestle is invaluable, both in the kitchen and in the circle. The pestle effectively grinds herbs and fuses ingredients together, while the heavy stone construction of the mortar makes a sturdy base. It is best to get a mortar that is wide enough to accommodate larger mixes and spells.

Note: You will need to keep a separate mortar and pestle for use in the circle—and never use it in the kitchen—in order to prevent cross-contamination with any toxic or otherwise poisonous substances used in magic. Better to be safe than sickened!

CHARGING
MAGICAL INGREDIENTS

J UST AS RITUAL TOOLS ARE CONSECRATED, MAGICAL INGRE-
dients, such as candles, herbs, crystals, and oils, are cleared of
any undesired energy and charged for their particular purposes.
There are many methods for clearing and charging spell ingredients of all kinds.

One of the simplest and most effective ways is to expose the
item(s) to moonlight or sunlight for several hours. These natural
sources of light both cleanse unwanted energy and charge them
with magical energy at the same time. You can also smudge items,
lay them on a pentacle slab or a quartz crystal, or ring a bell over
them.

Whichever method you choose, it's important to have a clear
focus on your magical goal when you charge the object. Hold the
item in your hands for a few moments while visualizing the desired
result, and then let it charge in the light of the sun or the moon.

TABLES OF
CORRESPONDENCE

Tables of correspondence illustrate various qualities and associations of tangible objects like crystals and stones, herbs and oils, and intangible phenomena like colors, months, astrological signs, and even days of the week.

Included here are a few brief tables of correspondence. You can consult these when exploring options for ritual, spellwork, and other Craft activity. Be sure to research further, however—there are countless tables of correspondence with much more detailed information than is presented in this brief guide.

CRYSTALS & OTHER GEMSTONES

TABLES OF CORRESPONDENCE

CRYSTAL	COLOR	USES
AMETHYST	Violet	Sharpens mental focus and intuition, clears sacred space
BLOODSTONE	Green with flecks of red/gold	Promotes physical healing, fertility, and abundance
CARNELIAN	Red/orange	Wards off negative energies, inspires courage
CITRINE	Yellow	Aids self-confidence, renewal, useful dreams
HEMATITE	Silver/gray/shiny black	Strengthens willpower and confidence, helps with problem solving
LAPIS LAZULI	Blue/dark blue	Helps with meditation, altered consciousness, divination
MOONSTONE	White/pale blue	Used in Goddess rituals, good for intuition and wisdom
QUARTZ CRYSTAL	White/clear	Promotes healing, clarity, spiritual development
ROSE QUARTZ	Pink	Promotes emotional healing, love and friendship
TIGER'S EYE	Brown/tan/gold with bands of black	Protection, energy

TABLES OF CORRESPONDENCE

COLOR	RED	ORANGE	YELLOW	GREEN
QUALITIES	Passion, courage, strength, intense emotions	Energy, attraction, vitality, stimulation	Intellect, inspiration, imagination, knowledge	Abundance, growth, wealth, renewal, balance
MAGICAL USES	Love, physical energy, health, willpower	Adaptability to sudden changes, encouragement, power	Communication, confidence, divination, study	Prosperity, employment, fertility, health, good luck
ELEMENTAL AND OTHER ASSOCIATIONS	Fire, South, Mars, Aries	Mercury, Gemini	Air, East, Sun, Leo	Earth, North, Venus, Libra and Taurus

BLUE	INDIGO	VIOLET	BLACK	WHITE
Peace, truth, wisdom, protection, patience	Emotion, fluidity, insight, expressiveness	Spirituality, wisdom, devotion, peace, idealism	Dignity, force, stability, protection	Banishing and releasing negative energies, transformation, enlightenment
Healing, psychic ability, harmony in the home, understanding	Meditation, clarity of purpose, spiritual healing, self-mastery	Divination, enhancing nurturing qualities, balancing sensitivity	Banishing and releasing negative energies, transformation, enlightenment	Cleansing, clarity, establishing order, spiritual growth and understanding
Water, West, Jupiter, Sagittarius	Saturn and Neptune, Capricorn and Pisces	Uranus and Moon, Aquarius and Cancer	Saturn and Pluto, Capricorn and Scorpio	Spirit (the Fifth Element), Mercury and Moon, Virgo

MAGICAL ESSENTIAL OILS

TABLES OF CORRESPONDENCE

ESSENTIAL OIL	GENERAL MAGICAL USES
Bergamot	Promotes energy, success, prosperity
Cinnamon	Increases psychic connections, promotes healing, success, luck
Clove	Protection, courage, banishing negative energies, cleanses auras
Eucalyptus	Healing and purification
Frankincense	Relieves stress, aids meditation, brings heightened spiritual awareness
Jasmine	Strengthens intuition and inspiration, promotes sensuality and love
Lavender	Healing, cleansing, removing anxiety
Patchouli	Prosperity, lust, physical energy
Rose	Love, peace, enhancing beauty
Sandalwood	Clears negativity, promotes balanced energy flow
Ylang-Ylang	Promotes happiness, calms anger, enhances sexual attraction

MAGICAL HERBS
TABLES OF CORRESPONDENCE

HERB	GENERAL MAGICAL USES
Basil	Fosters loving vibrations, protection, wards off negativities in a home
Bay Leaf	Protection, purification, healing, strength, good fortune, money, and success
Chamomile	Brings love, healing, relieves stressful situations
Cinnamon	Love, luck, prosperity, success, raises spiritual vibrations
Dandelion	Divination, interaction with the spirit world, wishes
Elecampane	Protection, luck, dispels negative vibration, plant spirit communication
Hibiscus	Divination, dreams, love, and lust
Lavender	Love, peace, restful sleep, clairvoyance, happiness, healing, money, passion, protection, relief from grief, longevity, meditation
*Mugwort	Psychic powers, protection, increases lust and fertility *Do not ingest, and do not handle if pregnant
Nutmeg	Money, prosperity, good luck, protection
Rosemary	Love and lust spells, promotes healthy rest
Sage	Longevity, wisdom, protection, dispels negative energy
Star Anise	Luck, spiritual connection, psychic and magical power
Thyme	Attracts loyalty, affection, psychic abilities
Valerian	Protection, drives away negativity, purifies sacred space
Yarrow	Healing, divination, love, promotes courage and confidence

NEXT STEPS

NOW THAT YOU HAVE A BASIC GROUNDING IN THE CORE beliefs and practices of modern Wicca, you may be wondering where to go from here. Should you get yourself an altar and some ritual tools in time for the next Sabbat? Should you start researching the most effective spells for improvements you'd like to see in your life? While there's nothing wrong with doing either of these things, know that there is much more to learn about Wicca than what has been presented in this introductory guide.

In part four, you'll find some advice for moving forward with your study of the Craft and deepening your connection to the natural world. You'll also find an example of a Wiccan ritual and a simple spell that you can try as part of your continued learning.

ADVICE FOR ASPIRING WICCANS & WITCHES

FINDING YOUR WAY
INTO THE CRAFT

A S WE HAVE SEEN, WICCA DIFFERS FROM OTHER RELIGIONS in many respects, not least of which is its lack of centralized structure and official, authoritative texts that spell out specific forms of practice for all to follow. What's more, Wicca doesn't tend to actively seek new practitioners. This leaves it up to individuals who might be interested in the Craft to find information and possible connections with others in the Wiccan community.

Thankfully, the Internet has made it far easier than it used to be for Wiccans and Witches to find and post information and communicate with each other. Nonetheless, there's no clear-cut path to lead you exactly where you want to be, aside from your own intuition.

This final section of *Wicca for Beginners* offers a few possible steps you can take in the direction of building and developing a spiritual practice. You'll find not only the usual (and very important!) advice to continue an active study of the Craft, but also ways to start incorporating your sense of spirituality into more of your daily life. At the end, you'll find an example of how you might celebrate a Sabbat, along with a simple, but effective, spell to promote balance and abundance in your life.

READ AND REACH OUT

THE BEST WAY TO GET STARTED ON BUILDING AND DEVELoping a spiritual practice is to read widely about Wicca and/or other forms of Paganism. A short list of suggested references is at the end of this guide on pages 154–55, and there is an enormous amount of information available in bookstores and online, much of it from venerable and experienced sources. New voices with new visions for the Craft also continue to emerge.

If you read widely enough, you'll encounter conflicting beliefs and advice—and this is a good thing, as it allows you to develop your own personal understanding of the forces and phenomena at work in Wicca and Witchcraft. Follow what resonates with you at the deepest level.

If a ritual, spell, a particular philosophy, or any other idea doesn't appeal to you, leave it out of your developing practice and keep seeking more information that feels "right." Most Wiccans and Witches will tell you that it takes a long time of study and observation to create an authentic personal relationship with the Craft.

If you're looking to connect with others—and depending where you live—there may be a local coven, circle, or other such group that you could join, or at least approach for information and advice. If there is a spiritual or "New Age" store in your area, odds are that someone there will know of any existing groups. You can also check event listings online, in local newspapers, or use other community resources to connect with others.

Finally, you can send out an intention to the Universe to help bring the people you're looking for into your life. It may be that a group near you is looking for someone new to join them, and you will end up in the right place at the right time to serendipitously meet one of their members! You can also always start your own "study group" to find like-minded souls who also want to learn more about Wicca, Witchcraft, and/or other forms of Paganism.

CHOOSING A PATH: COVEN, CIRCLE, SOLITARY, OR ECLECTIC?

FOR THOSE INTERESTED IN WORKING WITH OTHER WICCANS and Witches, covens and circles can be a good way to get solid training and advice from experienced practitioners. The terms *coven* and *circle* can be confusing for beginners, as they are often used interchangeably. They are not, however, the same thing.

A circle is usually a fairly informal group whose members may get together to discuss and learn about the Craft, and who may experiment with different kinds of ritual and spellwork. They may or may not meet for Sabbats and/or Esbats, depending on the collective wishes of the group. Depending on how "open" the group is, there may be many members, some of whom drop in and out as it suits them, or just a few regularly involved friends. The structure of a circle is generally loose and doesn't require official initiation or involve an established hierarchy.

A coven is more structured and usually has one or more established leaders, such as a High Priestess and/or High Priest, especially in Traditional Wicca. Covens meet for Sabbats and Esbats and members are expected to attend these gatherings, as the participation of each person is important to the ritual. Initiation is generally required, although it's fairly unlikely that someone brand-new to Wicca will be quickly initiated into a coven, for a few reasons.

One is that covens are generally small groups, with seven being considered an ideal number, and there's a tradition of not going over thirteen members. (Often, if there's enough interest to push a coven past thirteen, one member will depart to start a new, separate coven.) So, depending on how well established a coven is, there may simply not be any openings. Secondly, coven members want potential new initiates to have spent a good deal of time studying before inviting them to participate in formal ritual. Finally, since the bonds formed between coven members are strong and fairly intimate, the question of whether someone's personality and general energy are a good fit is an important one.

For those who don't live near any covens or circles, or who simply prefer not to incorporate a social element into their experience of the Craft, the life of a solitary or eclectic Witch can be just as meaningful and rewarding. Perhaps you'd rather get to know the spiritual and magical dimensions of the Universe on your own for some time, and then consider reaching out to like-minded others, or perhaps you're just born to be a solo practitioner. No matter what, there's a plethora of informational sources out there to guide you along the way.

The terms *solitary* and *eclectic* may sometimes be used interchangeably, as there can be a lot of overlap, but the distinctions are worth pointing out here. *Solitary* refers to the practice of Wicca or

Witchcraft on one's own, without any group experience, such as a coven or circle. Wiccans who belong to covens may (and often do) still practice on their own, along with their participation in coven work, but a solitary Wiccan or Witch always works alone. A solitary Witch can still intentionally follow what is commonly agreed to be"Traditional Wicca, such as Gardnerian, British Traditional Wicca, or another "lineage-based" tradition, and those who do so tend to identify as solitary rather than eclectic.

Eclectic is a description for Witches who don't follow a single, specific tradition and instead borrow and blend ideas, methods, practices, etc. from a variety of sources, and may also (and often do) invent their own. Some covens also consider themselves to be eclectic, although this tends to irritate members of traditional covens. It's worth remembering here that even the earliest recognized forms of Traditional Wicca were essentially borrowed, blended, and self-"invented."

LIVING THE
WHEEL OF THE YEAR

WICCA AND WITCHCRAFT ARE ROOTED IN A RELATIONSHIP with nature and its various expressions in plant and animal life, the elements, and the turning of the seasons. The living, breathing Divine Mind is vibrantly present in nature, perhaps more obviously so than in most of the human-made, modern, "developed world." Those interested in Wicca and Witchcraft will benefit from consciously observing the natural world around them and developing a more intentional relationship with it.

Witches who live in climates with four distinct seasons (Spring, Summer, Autumn, and Winter) have an excellent opportunity to closely observe the Wheel of the Year. Sabbats are the best time to note the changes on the Earth and in the sky, and Esbats also provide occasions for marking the seasons' effects on our everyday lives. The more you pay attention to the space" in between seasons," the more the movement of the Earth becomes apparent—even in Winter.

If you live in a climate with less seasonal variety, or even none at all to speak of, you can still observe the effects of natural forces in subtle ways. The sun still casts different qualities of light throughout the day. The air tends to change just before a rain. Becoming practiced in the habit of observing small details in your natural environment helps cultivate your openness to the unseen energies inherent in the entire Universe.

If you can, go out for walks, hikes, picnics, etc., in places with soil and vegetation. Or go swimming, canoeing, or rock skipping across a pond. Build a snowman or sculpt your own creation in snow. Do whatever you can to spend some quality time outdoors on a regular basis.

If you live in a very urban environment and have little in the way of access to natural areas, you can still create ways to interact with the underlying forces of the Universe. Parks can be suitable, but so can indoor plants and windowsill gardens. You can grow herbs for magical use and healing as well as cooking. Open a window at sunrise and study whatever you can see of the sky. Stand in the rain for a minute and embrace the feeling of it on your skin. Even nature shows and photographs or art that depict natural scenes can help put you in touch, as well as recordings of nature sounds and meditation music.

When Sabbats come around, make a point of gathering a few of the seasonal gifts of the Earth—flower petals in Spring months, leaves shed from deciduous trees in Autumn, pine needles from evergreens in Winter. Use these in ritual, or simply as decorations on your kitchen table or someplace else where you'll see them often. As you practice these ways of observing the Wheel of the Year, you'll find your relationship with the seasons (even your least favorite ones) becoming more attuned and rooted in gratitude.

DEITIES
AND THE DIVINE

S EEKING AND ATTAINING A SPIRITUAL RELATIONSHIP WITH the Triple Goddess, Cernunnos, Diana or any other of the many deities from around the ancient world can be a very effective way to enter the Craft, and many people find their experience to be deepened and sharpened through the practice of more traditional, structured forms of Wicca. But some newcomers to Wicca and Witchcraft are unsure about the notion of "worshipping" deities and may feel strange about searching for one or more specific gods or goddesses with whom to form relationships or alignments. Borrowing from older traditions in this respect may not quite feel like an authentic approach to a spiritual search.

It's true that it takes time to find and cultivate an interest in and a relationship with a deity you weren't aware of until recently, and people who were raised in monotheistic religions can struggle even more with integrating the concept of polytheism. But it's also true that you don't absolutely *have* to incorporate a belief in or a relationship with any specific form of the divine. You might just work with the idea of a Goddess and a God, or even less definitively identified energies of the Universe.

Faith and belief are far more often developed and cultivated over time than immediately attained. Make an effort to study and seek yours, but go at your own pace, and trust your intuition. No one can tell you you're not a true Wiccan or Witch because your relationship with the divine doesn't match their experience.

(Well, some might, but in a religion with so many variations, it's only natural that some will quibble about the details.) There's no intermediary between you and the Universe, and there are as many paths to the Divine as there are people who seek it.

If you do see connecting with deities as a possible part of your path, start doing some research. Read about them—in Wiccan books, in ancient myths, in poetry, in history books. (Watch out for bias in the history books, however—in the Judeo-Christian world, the deities of polytheism are often negatively and erroneously portrayed.) You may discover, as some Witches do, that a deity will actually find you, through images, dreams, seemingly "random" events or coincidences, or in other ways.

MEDITATION AND VISUALIZATION

PREPARING FOR RITUAL AND MAGICAL WORK INVOLVES accessing a beneficial altered state of mind that allows for both openness and focus. Many traditions practice specific meditation and visualization techniques to strengthen this ability and call on it when needed.

You can find information on meditation in Witchcraft or many other spiritual traditions. Seek out different kinds of meditation and practices that work best for you. If nothing else, be sure to set aside time and space for solitude and reflection, preferably every day, but definitely before ritual and spellwork.

T HIS FAIRLY SIMPLE RITUAL IS OFFERED AS ONE EXAMPLE OUT
of countless possibilities. It's designed for solitary practice but
could certainly be adapted for use with a coven. Like most rituals,
it can be tailored to your intuition, preferences, or circumstances.
(It can also be replicated for other Sabbats, with changes made to
seasonal items, candle colors, etc.)

It's a bit pared down compared to a full formal Wiccan ritual,
but it incorporates many of the core components, in order to give
you a sense of the process without being overwhelmed by detail. If
you don't wish to incorporate any practical magic component, feel
free to skip the spell candle and the words of intention.

Remember that if you don't have everything listed below, you
don't have to go out and buy it—you can substitute, simplify, and
improvise as you wish. However, you should at least have a candle
or two, and some form of representation of the current season to
serve as points of focus for your energy.

In Wicca, the Sabbat at the Autumn Equinox is also known as
Mabon. This is a time for celebrating the abundance of the harvest, and for observing the balancing point of equal day and equal
night that occurs at this point on the Wheel of the Year. A common
theme to focus on at this Sabbat is gratitude: to the Sun for making
the harvest possible, and to the Earth for yielding enough abundance to carry us through the Winter months.

The end of Summer is also a time when the abundance of the
Earth begins to die back in order to make room for new growth
in the next cycle. This is an opportunity to begin turning inward
and looking forward to a more restful time. We can use this
moment to identify the things in our lives that aren't needed

anymore—whether it is too much "stuff," an old habit we've wanted to break, or anything else that we'd like to let go of.

As we feel the seasons shift from the light to the dark half of the year, we can set intentions for balance in any aspect of our lives. As you prepare for the ritual, meditate on these themes and notice what comes to mind. See this opportunity to gain insight into an aspect of your life that you may not have been conscious of before.

═══ RECOMMENDED ITEMS ═══

Seasonal representations such as late summer crops, especially corn and squash, apples, seeds, and/or marigolds.

CANDLES:
1 red, 1 white, and 1 dark green spell candle, and any others in autumn colors you wish to include.

Pentacle

Chalice

INCENSE AND/OR OILS:
Frankincense, sandalwood, pine, rosemary, chamomile

STONES:
Jade, carnelian, lapis lazuli

HERBS:
Sage, hawthorn, cedar

Any other ritual tools you wish to include

+ Decorate your altar (or other ritual space) with representations of the season and lay out your ritual tools and magical ingredients. You can do this in whatever way is most visually pleasing, or you can follow any traditional pattern that appeals to you.

+ One way is to place the white candle on the left for the Goddess, the red candle on the right for the God, the pentacle to the North and the cup to the West. A candle can be placed in the South—this can be the spell candle, if you're using it, or another candle. Incense or oils can be placed in the East. (If it's not practical to place burning incense right on the altar, you can place it somewhere nearby in the Eastern Quarter of the circle.) Any crystals, sprigs of herbs, or additional ritual tools can be placed around the edges of the altar or wherever they seem to "want" to be.

+ Take some time trying out different arrangements. You'll soon get a sense of what looks and feels right for you.

+ If you're casting a circle, make sure you have everything you're using for the ritual, and then decide how large your circle will need to be.

+ Mark the cardinal directions with candles or other items first, and then, if you wish, use sea salt, sprinkled herbs, tea lights, or stones to mark out the rest of the circle.

+ Charge the circle with intention for creating a sacred space by slowly walking clockwise around it from the inside. As you walk, "draw" the circle again by pointing with your wand, athame, or index finger, visualizing the energetic connection between your body and the circle's edge. You are creating a place of higher, more powerful energy than will exist on the outside of the circle. This is an act that takes practice and learning. Again, it is not strictly necessary, but it is a time-honored part of Wiccan tradition that many find to be integral.

- If you wish, call the quarters by turning to stand in each cardinal direction, starting with North and moving clockwise. Verbally recognize each direction by name and its associated element and ask for its energy to come into your circle. You are already incorporating symbols of the Elements with the pentacle (Earth), the incense or oil (Air), the candles (Fire), and the chalice (Water) so you could hold each of these items as you greet the Elements.

- Next, light the red and white candles and invite the God and Goddess—the balanced forces of male and female divine energy—to be present with you in the celebration.

- Spend some time reflecting on the abundance you've experienced in the past season. Identify a minimum of seven things you are grateful for and state what they are out loud. They can be small or large things—whatever you feel truly grateful for at this time. Then, ask for any help you need with establishing balance in an area of your life, maintaining security, and/or letting go of something in your life that is no longer serving you. You can write all of this out in advance to help you stay on track, or you can simply speak in the moment from your heart, improvising as you go along. You can also consult other sources on Wicca to find words that would be appropriate for this ritual. All that matters is that you resonate genuinely with what you are saying.

- If you're using the spell candle, rub a drop or two of essential oil into it, or just hold it in your hands for a few moments. Visualize yourself feeling secure, emotionally balanced, and grateful for the abundance in your life. Out loud, state this vision in whatever way seems most natural to you. You might simply say, "I have all that I need and more. I am in a state of healthy balance in all things." Or, you might zero in your focus more specifically, for example: "I have the money I need for [your purpose]."

When you've formulated and stated your magical intention, light the green candle as you "seal" the work with a final phrase. Many Witches use one of the following: "So let it be," "So mote it be," "Blessed Be," or "It is done." Whatever you choose, be sure to consciously release your intentions into the higher realms where they can be transformed and manifest.

Watch the flame for a few moments, feeling the positive energies rise within you and all around you in this sacred space. When you're ready, thank the Goddess and God, as well as the Elements, for their presence and attention to your ritual.

Then, close the circle by walking around it counter-clockwise, visualizing its energy dispersing into the Universe. Don't leave any candles unattended but do let the spell candle burn out on its own, if at all possible.

Over the next few weeks, continue the practice of recognizing abundance and expressing gratitude. You may also notice any seeming imbalances in your life or well-being and decide what you can do to correct them. If you do so, you will see that the Universe will support you!

CONCLUSION

I T'S QUITE A CHALLENGE TO CREATE A TRULY ENCOMPASSING beginner's guide to Wicca. Perhaps more than in any other religion, its widely diverse practitioners will interpret its many facets differently—in some cases, *very* differently. As you read and study further, and as you meet and interact with fellow practitioners, you might find that some people's views vary wildly from those presented here. Nonetheless, the goal of this guide has been to provide a general orientation to Wiccan beliefs and practices from an unbiased perspective.

When you are just starting out, you are encouraged to read and learn as much as possible, so your initial beliefs are bound to be shaped by the books and other sources you encounter. Over time, as you begin to embrace Wicca in your daily life, you may have certain epiphanies that re-shape your approach to your practice. What resonates with you on one day might be very different from where you are on day 100, and could be a world apart from your views and beliefs on day 1,000. Wicca is truly a lifelong journey, and even after decades you will still find yourself learning new things.

One of the best things about Wicca is that your interpretations, views, and beliefs are highly personal. Wicca has no dogma and no official authority that can tell you whether or not you're "doing it right." You need only to follow your heart and sit in the light of that which resonates within it. You will find yourself growing and changing in miraculous ways when the light of the Goddess and the God is shining upon you.

Blessed Be.

ACKNOWLEDGMENTS

MY DEEPEST THANKS TO MY BIRTH FAMILY AND MY CHOSEN family for their eternal love and support. To Lana, for knowing about journeys. To Denise and Justin, for crash courses in manifestation. And to Sally, for the friendship of so many lifetimes.

Thanks to editor Barbara Berger and the rest of the team at Sterling for being such creative visionaries in bringing this book into being: art director Elizabeth Lindy for the beautiful cover design; interior art directors Kevin Ullrich and Christine Heun; Sharon Jacobs for the stunning interior design conception, direction, and layout; production editor Michael Cea; and production manager Krista-Lise Endahl.

SUGGESTIONS FOR FURTHER READING

HISTORY OF TRADITIONAL WICCA

Adler, Margot. *Drawing Down the Moon: Witches, Druids, Goddess-Worshippers, and Other Pagans in America*. New York: Viking, 1979.

Buckland, Raymond. *Buckland's Complete Book of Witchcraft*. St. Paul: Llewellyn, 1986, 2002.

——. *Witchcraft From the Inside: Origins of the Fastest Growing Religious Movement in America*. St. Paul: Llewellyn, 1971, 1975, 1995.

Gardner, Gerald B. *Witchcraft Today*. New York: Citadel Press, 1954, 2004.

——. *The Meaning of Witchcraft*. Boston: Weiser Books, 1959, 2004.

Leek, Sybil. *The Complete Art of Witchcraft: Penetrating the Secrets of White Magic*. New York: Signet, 1973.

Valiente, Doreen. *Where Witchcraft Lives*. London: Aquarian, 1962.

CONTEMPORARY WICCA AND WITCHCRAFT

Cabot, Laurie, with Tom Cowan. *Power of the Witch: The Earth, the Moon, and the Magical Path to Enlightenment.* New York: Delta, 1990.

Conway, D. J. *Celtic Magic.* St. Paul, MN: Llewellyn, 1990.

Cunningham, Scott. *Wicca: A Guide for the Solitary Practitioner.* St. Paul, MN: Llewellyn, 1989.

Dugan, Ellen. *Natural Witchery: Intuitive, Personal & Practical Magick.* St. Paul, MN: Llewellyn, 2007.

Farrar, Janet, and Steward Farrar. *Eight Sabbats for Witches.* Blaine, WA: Phoenix, 1981, 1988.

SCIENCE AND MAGIC

Bentov, Itzhak. *Stalking the Wild Pendulum: On the Mechanics of Consciousness.* Rochester, VT: Destiny, 1977, 1988.

Briggs, John C., and F. David Peat, *Looking Glass Universe: The Emerging Science of Wholeness.* New York: Simon & Schuster, 1986.

Capra, Fritjof. *The Tao of Physics: An Exploration of the Parallels Between Modern Physics and Eastern Mysticism.* Boston: Shambhala, 2010.

Peat, F. David. Synchronicity: *The Bridge Between Matter and Mind.* New York: Bantam, 1987.

PICTURE CREDITS

INDEX

ABOUT THE AUTHOR

LISA CHAMBERLAIN is the successful author of more than twenty books on Wicca and magic, including *Wicca for Beginners*, *Wicca Herbal Magic*, and *Wiccan Kitchen*. Her Wiccan experience has evolved over years from a traditional practice to more eclectic explorations. Her focus is on positive magic that promotes self-empowerment for the good of the whole.

You can find out more at:
wiccaliving.com